JOURNEY TO HOME

Quintessential Therapy and Beyond

To my friend, Brigitte:
May your journey lead
you to home.
warmly,
Rachel

Rachel B. Aarons, MSW, PhD

Published by Journey Press, Santa Barbara, CA 93101

Printed in the United States of America. All rights reserved.

Copyright © 2009 Rachel Aarons

ISBN: 978-0-9842327-0-3

Design by Laurence T. Brockway

Cover art by David Aarons

Dedication

This book is dedicated to my sons,
Kieran and David,
who mean everything to me.

I hope that the writing of this book
played a part in their becoming
the remarkable human beings they are
and that the reading of it may offer
inspiration in their life journeys.

Contents

Introduction

This is a book about a journey. It is a journey that is intensely personal and at the same time universal. If I didn't believe that it was universal, or at least widely applicable, I wouldn't have written about it. That voice in my head, the one that keeps rattling on: "Who cares what you think?" "Who cares even less what you went through?" "Who do you think you *are??*" That voice might have drowned out my resolve. It might have convinced me to retreat in silence, tucking my pretensions out of view.

After all, to write a book, I imagined, one would have to be stunningly creative, courageous, or smart. Or at least, one would have to have accomplished some world-shattering, momentous feat that awaited history's notice. None of this applies to me.

At times it still seems remarkable to me that people do relate to what I have written and do find meaning in my story. For I am nobody of extraordinary or special importance. And this is exactly the point. It dawned on me that it is my commonality with others, my humanness that I have to offer. And my willingness to share it with you.

Who reads a book on the therapeutic journey? Who am I to picture out there?

Presumably you are people who have an interest in human development and are perhaps clients of therapy or therapists yourselves. (Hopefully, these are not mutually exclusive categories.) If you are reading this book, you may be looking for some understanding of your own process of healing. You may be seeking a structure to give meaning to your life and perhaps to provide a direction for change.

A structure of this sort would have to be theoretical in the sense that it would provide an intellectually valid way of interpreting a whole range of life experience reaching beyond individual autobiography to a general human level. To be viable, this theoretical structure would have to be intimately connected to the issues we struggle with in our daily lives, in our most important relationships, and in our work.

I believe the hope for connection lies in the presentation of *lived truth*. The theory I present is, by its nature, very abstract. The truth, however, is very concrete. In the bridge between these two, hopefully, you will find a meaningful connection.

As a therapist, I have a deep and compelling interest in people and their lives. My daily commitment to therapy is the reality behind every page. I've spent many, many hours closeted in a tiny room, sharing with one person after another their profoundly moving stories. These were people who had come to heal, moved by some anxiety, frustration or pain in their lives. They came to me assuming that I knew something about how they could heal. They told me about their pain and often they did heal. But how did it happen? Perhaps I would sound knowledgeable and they would be grateful but what had really happened? It was, at bottom, a mystery.

In my evolution as a therapist, each theoretical framework I embraced gave its own answer to this question, but I noticed that people kept healing even though I went from one theory to another. Each methodology I employed claimed that *it* was the way that worked but, again, it appeared that people were progressing equally well no matter what the methodology.

Was it some magic I possessed? Was there some great wisdom in me that opened the way? If so, I had to admit I did not know how to define it. Nor could I use it to hasten my own healing. There were times when I would look with an admiration bordering on envy at the way my clients would resolve issues that I remained stuck with. If I could help them, why couldn't I help myself? Or did it have anything to do with my helping? Could it be that I was essentially a witness to a process they were undergoing that had little, if anything, to do with me?

If there was such a process, I wanted to know more about it so that I could get on with my own work, both as a therapist and in my own healing. It is my belief that we who are therapists are often doing this work because of a need for healing in our own lives. Yet isn't it curious that we hardly ever talk about our own work, our need for healing, or how we heal?

In our consulting rooms and in the therapeutic literature, we rarely offer more than a few passing remarks about our own struggles. We always talk about *other* people. We focus on the client. We offer case studies and case examples. We are ashamed to acknowledge that we are engaged in a process of healing ourselves. We think we would lose credibility.

It is a sad comment on the field of psychotherapy that we believe we need to hide behind a mask of invulnerability, that it has become a daring venture to use frankly autobiographical material in a book about therapy and that, rather than personal experience being a confirmation of one's intimate knowledge of human struggle, it could be seen as a potential basis for discreditation.

It is my intention to challenge this belief. This book, in its presentation of deeply personal material rather than anonymous case material, constitutes that challenge.

I would urge that this new level of disclosure by a therapist be regarded as a necessary step in the direction of greater honesty in psychotherapy, a direction that I believe is long overdue. Many may, certainly the orthodox will, disagree with me - likely in unflattering terms. But, fortunately, there is no better training for the challenge of standing one's ground in the face of discreditation than growing up in a dysfunctional family. This book will show in depth why this is so.

I invite you, then, to join me in this journey. It will take place on two parallel tracks, one theoretical, the other personal. It will be clear from the change of typeface when I have switched tracks. As I develop the logical structure of the therapeutic process, I will interweave personal anecdotes that are intended to illustrate and clarify the points in the theory. As these points are connected in one coherent whole, so the anecdotes are connected in one story, which is a single life.

This journey could be characterized as a "victim's" journey. Let me say right off that I am not unaware that in using the term "victim" rather than the more popular term "survivor", I may ruffle some sensibilities. While this particular ruffling is not my objective, nonetheless I take this risk because I believe it is imperative to explore in depth the process of victimization and, to do so, we need to have a term for the correlate of the abuser in the dynamic of an abusive relationship. If, as I will maintain, the roles of victim and abuser are both inevitable and inevitably reciprocal, then we all, on some level, need to come to terms with the victim in ourselves.

But we do not need to stay there. This book does not advocate resignation. It is, on the contrary, a call to arms. The goal is to find a way to transcend the victim position, to overcome both abuse of ourselves and of others in order to learn how to love. If this is a victim's journey, it is every bit as much a journey *out* of victimization. We will be most empowered to move out of the victim position when we can name it and recognize it for what it is.

Nothing in my life story has been invented or altered to prove a point. My constant consideration has been to represent, as closely as possible, the truth as I experienced it, while realizing that it is always *my* viewpoint, *my* truth.

It is not my intention to blame, castigate, or condemn anyone. Quite the opposite: the learning of this entire endeavor is the appreciation of our humanness. Ultimately, the goal of writing this book and the goal of therapy are the same - the development of a sympathetic witness who can both see *and* love the self.

Part One

Self and Other:
The Logic of the
Therapeutic Journey

" To be really human is the thing that
                most humans don't want to be."

A.H. Almaas

To begin the journey, I want to talk about a process. It is the process of therapy: that is, it is the process that is engaged whenever transformation or healing takes place, no matter what the methodology.

I believe that there is an underlying process that is common to diverse therapeutic systems — the elephant that is being touched by our blind hands — and that this underlying process is logical.

To say that it is logical means that if you look at its structure, you will see that it has certain essential features which I call "principles", some of which are definitional and some explanatory, and that it follows a pattern through time in what may be termed cycles or even a spiral.

If I am right, this process should appear strikingly familiar to you and you should recognize these principles as true and maybe even obvious. Otherwise, I am wrong in my formulation. Therefore, I would expect to elicit responses like: "yes, of course;" "I knew that;" or "that's what happened to me." My objective is to articulate that which is known and common, not to offer something radically new and different.

Consequently, it would not be a significant criticism of this point of view to argue that it lacks novelty or originality. In fact, the contrary would be the case. What I am offering claims to be a phenomenology of our human experience, a form of universal or archetypal journey, and one that we can all, on some level, recognize.

I maintain that although there are different languages of therapy, and perhaps different routes to get to the same goal, the fundamental process is the same and is what makes therapy "work", when it does.

Psychotherapy is not the only form of thought that is concerned with this process. It is depicted in mythology and religion, in literature and art, in fairy tales and folk songs. But psychotherapy is most distinctively concerned with this process in that it is our modern style of journey-making. It is,

as Jung suggested, modern man's search for a soul.[1]

The fundamental process of therapy is, I believe, a process of becoming oneself - that old cliché which, I maintain, is true and accurate as to what occurs. But how can we understand the meaning of this process? How is it possible to "become oneself?"

In order to make sense of the notion of becoming oneself, we have to make sense of the notion of not being oneself which lies behind it. How can I become myself unless I am, in some sense, not myself? But if I am not myself, then who am I?

On this point, John Welwood says:

Process-oriented psychotherapy, as I practice it, has a larger purpose than just coping, controlling, or feeling better. It's about connecting with the truth of who we really are. To understand how therapeutic inquiry can help us connect more deeply with ourselves, we need to recognize the nature of the basic distress or "dis-ease" that lies at the root of all our psychological problems. We have all turned away from certain areas of our experience that caused us pain as we were growing up - such as our anger, our need for love, our vulnerability, our will, our sexuality - and have withdrawn our awareness from them. [2]

It is in the recovery of these lost areas that the process of therapy can serve, according to Welwood, as a bridge to the reintegration of the self.

Clearly, therapy would not need to reintegrate the self were it not already fragmented and damaged. Recovery of self implies a prior loss of self. Integration presupposes disintegration.

Most of us acknowledge the possibility of not being ourselves. We say: "I was not myself today." "I can't be myself with you (my husband, my boss, my father, my mother)."

1 Jung, Carl: *Modern Man in Search of a Soul*, Harcourt, Brace & World, New York, first published in 1933.
2 Welwood, John: "Psychotherapy and the Power of Truth", *Yoga Journal*, May/June 1992.

"That person is not who s/he appears to be."

Yet if we stop to think about it, how can we make sense of this notion of not being who we are?

We have in our language a concept of denial in terms of which it makes sense to say that someone is "in denial" about themselves or denies a truth about themselves. It is not simply that they do not know the truth. It is that they know it but at the same time deny that they know it.

For example, one of my mother's frequent statements took the form "I'm not [fill in verb] ___ing but ..." For example: "I'm not criticizing but..." or "I'm not complaining but... " In such a statement my mother succeeded in accurately describing what she was about to do in the very process of denying that description.

If I pointed out that she was, in fact, [fill in verb] ____ing (e.g. criticizing, complaining), I would be soundly reprimanded for my perpetual misinterpretation of her. This misjudgment was proven definitively by the statement she had just made, saying that she was NOT!

The posture of self-righteousness that inevitably accompanied such pronouncements should not be dismissed as mere pretense on her part, nor as an unfortunately all-too-obvious attempt at deception. She was not being dishonest. She genuinely meant what she said. And she was utterly convinced of her own rightness.

It would be necessary to say, then, that the person in denial is simultaneously deceiving (or attempting to deceive) themselves.

The possibility of *self-deception* is, as the philosopher Jean Paul Sartre[3] noted, a remarkably curious phenomenon. It is easy to see how one person could deceive another person by keeping information secret or hidden. But it is not so easy to understand how information could be kept secret or hidden from oneself. Are there walls in the mind? Secret rooms?

---

3 Sartre, Jean Paul: *Being and Nothingness, A Phenomenological Essay on Ontology,* (translated by Hazel E. Barnes,) Citadel Press, New York, 1956, see section on "Bad Faith."

Compartments where information could be kept by oneself and yet away from oneself?

To be not oneself, to be in denial, and to deceive oneself all imply that it is possible for the self to be split and divided against itself.

Our principles have to begin, then, with the formation of the self and how the self can get split or damaged in the first place so that it later needs to be healed.

* * *

When I had just turned six years old, I was sent to a distant summer camp for two months. My sister insists I was five but, five or six, it amounts to much the same thing: I was very little. Camp Kawagama (pronounced Ka-wa-gama, with the emphasis on the second syllable) was situated seven hours' train ride from my home. As if the prospect of seven hours in a train wasn't daunting enough to stretch the imaginative capacity of a little girl who had never been away from home, the camp was on an island! It took another three-quarters of an hour by motor boat to get there. No matter how well I could swim at age five or six, it was clear there was no way to get home.

Not surprisingly, I was dreadfully homesick. I don't recall if any of the other children suffered as I did, but I know that I was in agony. I went to my sister's cabin and curled up in her bed, clinging to the scent of something familiar.

My sister was seven years older and, at first, she cradled me like the mother I wanted her to be. Everyone was sympathetic for a while but I was not about to let go. I still remember vividly how I clung to her and I hung on – for dear life.

They pulled me screaming and thrashing away from her bed and carried me crying and kicking away from her cabin. I was barred from going there again. I still remember standing at a distance staring at it wistfully. How inaccessible it seemed to me. Cabin 11 – the only one on stilts.

* * *

Our first principle is:

1. The self is formed in relationship.

This principle means that as far back as we go in the development of the self, we will encounter self in the context of other selves. There is no lone ego out there riding the range, fulfilling its solitary destiny on earth, the only living being against a backdrop of the setting sun. We are in this game together. It means that we cannot have a self in the absence of other selves; that is, in isolation. In particular, we need other beings like ourselves. Self requires other people.

This is true in the sense that the experience of limit to the self requires that which is other or not-self. Only in this way are we able to distinguish the me from the not-me. It is in the interaction with other people that the self gets defined as separate from that which is outside it. In order to define the self, we need boundaries that mark the distinction between self and not-self. In order to define boundaries, we need others.

The second principle states:

2. Boundaries are the interface of self and other in relationship.

This distinction between self and other is thought to occur as the infant learns to recognize that the whole universe is not itself. The breast walks away or is forced upon us. We come to realize that other people are independent and not under our control. This insight is frequently experienced with frustration and makes our babies howl - even when we occupy adult bodies.

Here at the core of the formation of the self, we discover

in germinal form the template for difficulties in relationship. We want others to fill us, to feed us, to keep us comfortable and satiated. We want security and comfort which comes from outside.

The glitch is: the outside is not under our control.

It is terrifying when we come to the realization that the possessor of our life supply can disappear in an instant, without warning, perhaps forever. We stave off conscious realization of this terror but we act it out.

This fear of being abandoned is a driving force underlying many of our interactions with others. We panic at the possibility of rejection. We hang on for dear life. We try in a multitude of complex and cunning ways to ensure that the other will be there for us, meeting our needs. Of course, the other will likely be doing the same thing, just as vigorously.

It has frequently been observed in marital therapy that the classic relationship between spouses takes the form of parent/child interaction. A recent example is the book *Dancing In the Dark* [4] in which the authors, Doug and Naomi Moseley, analyze mother/son and father/daughter patterns of relating in married couples.

If we believe that our significant other is as necessary to us as a parent is to a baby, then inevitably we will try to control the other to keep them in role. If we feel that the other is trying to control us and get us to parent them, we will probably resist. The ubiquitous control battles of the marital domain begin to make sense.

On a deeper more primordial level, it is not so much control of the other as obliteration of the distinction between self and other that we seek. We yearn to merge with the other, to dissolve the boundary between self and other in order to recreate that mythic primal fullness and unity. It is this deep yearning for union that is at the heart of romantic love, in its agony and its ecstasy.

---

4 Moseley, Doug and Naomi: *Dancing in the Dark: The Shadow Side of Intimate Relationships*, North Star Publications, Georgetown, Massachusetts, 1994.

We can hardly underestimate the extent of human suffering that is derived from this yearning. Perhaps if the universe poured into us unendingly in exactly the ways we wanted and needed, we would never know ourselves to be separate. But this is impossible. Inevitably there is a rupture; the harmony is shattered and our contentment is destroyed.

Even intra-uterine existence is not the uninterrupted bliss it is imagined to be when we are said to have a longing to go "back to the womb." In actuality, it can be a place of turbulence, tension, and apprehension. It can be a suffocating, stuck place, a place we return to repeatedly whenever we drop into hopelessness. Through the use of methods such as hypnotherapy and body work, we can re-experience our pain and our contraction against this pain going right back to the foetal state. Yet it is true that it is only through pain and contraction that limit will be introduced and only through the experience of limit that the self is born.

*   *   *

I tried to phone my mother. (I knew, even then, that there was no point in phoning my father.) I lined up dutifully every evening after supper waiting in line with my heart racing until the turns ran out and I would be sent away to try again the next day. Finally my turn came and the camp director, a child psychologist, spoke to my mom first. I don't know what she said but when I told my mother how miserable I was and that I wanted to come home, nothing ever came of it. I never called again and I stayed the whole two months.

I suspect they must have discussed the fact that I was homesick and concluded that it would just go away. It's as if by the act of giving it a name and a status of predictability, it became okay for them to ignore my pain. Imagine our treating medical symptoms that way! Or perhaps because I was a child, rather than seeing in the vulnerability of childhood the need for nurturance and protection, they saw it as a pain diminished, one that would pass away quickly and easily, one that didn't count.

The truth is that it never went away. It was a pain that was to be relived not only every day that summer but countless times in my life as the trauma of Camp Kawagama was reenacted again and again.

It was also the pain that woke me up to the utter helplessness of the human being. At five years old, I learned that I was entirely on my own.

I remember standing at the water's edge on an isolated spit of land called Rocky Point at the far end of the island staring across the unending expanse of waves, dazed by the terrible ache of my loneliness. It was the moment of my first suicidal thought, although it was sixteen or seventeen years before I acted on that thought. How many days and years of depression were accompanied by that aching emptiness, punctuated by the words from a forgotten poem: "If I cried, who among all heaven's angels would hear me?"[5]

Why didn't my mother hear me? Why didn't she care? If you knew her history, how she lost both her parents before the age of eight and was picked on by her siblings, how the one brother who was good to her and whom she adored died when he was twenty-two and she was seventeen, and her lifelong history of depression, perhaps you would understand her inability to respond to the loneliness of her child, both the one who was inside her and the one that was me.

* * *

The need for limit to the self is not new information in the psychological literature. It was known, for example, by Piaget[6]. But there is a further implication of the need for other which has come to occupy a new focus of attention in current

5 Rilke, Rainer Maria: *Duino Elegies*, (translated by David Young,) W.W. Norton & Company, New York, 1978, First Elegy, page 19. When I tracked down this forgotten source, the translation was slightly different than I had remembered, and repeated, all those years i.e. "If I cried out, who would hear me up there among the angelic orders?"
6 *The Essential Piaget*, (ed. Howard Gruber and J. Jacques Voneche,) Basic Books, New York, 1977.

psychology, for example in Object Relations theory[7]. It is the fact that we cannot have an image or sense of ourselves in isolation from other people. That is, in order to get an image of our self, we must have a reflection of the self from a point of view that is outside of and separate from the self. Therefore, others are necessary for us to have a self-image. We gain our picture of ourselves through the mirroring of others.

Hence the third principle states:

3. Self-image is the result of mirroring by the other.

We must pause to recognize that, through the mirroring process, something truly momentous is happening here, something that creates a fundamental change in the self.

Not only is the self becoming separated from the other and ushering in that deep yearning for reconnection which underscores the drama of relationship. But a further schism is occurring in which the self is becoming separated not only from the other but also, at the same time, from itself.

This internal schism is inevitable because, in order to have a sense of self, there must be a distance or separation within the self - what may be called a splitting process - between the I that senses or reflects and the I that is sensed or reflected upon. The process of splitting into subject and object is labeled in philosophical terminology as a "reflexive" process. It follows, then, that consciousness of self is a reflexive process that includes at least two levels - the self that is (the object level) and the self that looks at the self that is (the subject level).

In other words, for the self to have an image of itself, it must take itself as an object that can be reflected upon. It does this through the medium of the other by taking a perspective on itself as if it were an "other" to itself. In this basic phenomenological triangle, we become simultaneously

---

7 For an overview of Object Relations theory, see, for example, Cashdan, Sheldon: *Object Relations Therapy*, W.W. Norton, New York, 1988.

object to the other and object to ourselves. We forfeit the unity of our being in ourselves in the same moment as we forfeit the unity which we had with the other.

As the self turns itself into an object, it becomes capable of turning against itself, just as others can do. Herein lies the possibility for self-judgment, self-attack, and self-deception. The birth of consciousness of the self is the birth of a self, divided, containing within itself the possibility of becoming divided against itself.

* * *

Not only was it not okay to be miserable at camp, we were supposed to be thrilled. The point of view adopted by my parents and many like them in our upper middle class nouveau-riche neighborhood was that it was a privilege to be sent to such a camp. Since it was so expensive, (they reasoned) we were lucky to go.

I did not realize the grotesque irony of this perspective until a phrase in Joan Borysenko's book, Guilt is the Teacher, Love is the Lesson, caught my eye. Recounting her awful experience at a summer camp, she described the place as a "surrealistic concentration camp." Suddenly I had the image of thousands of well-to-do Jewish kids being herded into buses and trains and shipped off to camps every summer by parents who had just survived World War II. This was 1947 or 1948. In this bizarre twist of fate, the ultimate degradation had become a status symbol. Summer camp was the "in" thing.

It was the implicit duty of we the favored children who were fortunate enough to be sent there to reassure our parents that they were getting their money's worth by smiling broadly and acting suitably enthusiastic on Visitor's Day. Anything less than unreserved appreciation would have been seen by my parents as ingratitude of a most unforgivable sort. It also vindicated their two months of leisure spent, sans kids, at the golf club. After all, my father worked very hard as a furrier in the winter months and felt he deserved a relaxing summer. My mother did not want to be "a *golf widow"* so she followed suit. *I remember asking only once if I could stay home from camp that year and my mother's incredulous reply: "But all the kids will be going to camp! What would you do all day?" It was a given that I would be a camp every summer after that.*

Reflecting on this incident some years later, my sister remarked with the same tone of incredulity: "What made you think there was any alternative?" She had obviously surrendered to inevitability from the outset. This must have made it difficult for her to put up with a whining clinging little sister who would not give up. She promptly withdrew and quit trying. After that brief offering of solace, she became cold and inaccessible, thus establishing the ongoing pattern of our relationship. From then on, she treated me like I was, in some mysterious way I could never grasp, forever in the way, a nuisance, someone she could, at best, tolerate.

I felt the label "pain in the butt" long before the words emerged that finally clarified the sense of being unwelcome I had carried for years. A felt sense like a blue-grey watercolor wash that colored my life experience in its somber tones. What I missed entirely was the nuance of admiration that came with her declaration: "But what made you think there was anything different? Anything else that was possible in life?"

* * *

The splitting into subject and object which allows for the possibility of a self divided also allows the self to take up a position vis-à-vis itself - to see itself, as it were, from the outside. This possibility of viewing itself from the outside may be called a meta-level and is known in therapy as the witness position. To be a witness is to be able to view oneself with what Milton Erickson called open curiosity and what Welwood calls unconditional presence, that is: "the ability to remain open and inquisitive to our experience, without bias, agenda, or manipulation of any kind".[8] It is one of the primary tasks of the therapeutic process to develop this ability

8 Welwood, John: "Psychotherapy and the Power of Truth," *Yoga Journal*, May/June 1992

to occupy the witness position.

To move from the general to the particular - from the process of developing self-image in general to the particular self-image that each of us has - requires that we consider the distinctive mirroring which occurs in our family of origin. When a client comes into therapy, we know that the self before us has been formed by having been in a particular family and that our client's self-image will likewise have been formed by the reflection he or she got from being in that family. In this sense, all therapy is family of origin therapy, whether this is explicit or implicit in the process of therapy itself. The self that comes into therapy is thus the product of a relational history, and we will see this history reenacted in the present in each person's current relationships, including their relationship to their body, to God, and to the therapist.

What we discover is that mirroring is not a passive reflection but an active shaping and distortion of the self for two powerful reasons.

The first reason has to do with the fact that the "mirrors" themselves have been shaped and distorted by their own family histories. We are looking at a process in time, passing from generation to generation. Dysfunction produces dysfunction. We are victims of victims.

Our family members, because of their histories, have needs of us. They need us to be certain ways and they put pressure on us to be so. Threat of abandonment or withdrawal of love lie at the root of all pressure. Family members see us through the medium of their own needs of us, not dispassionately, as we are. To perceive another not as they are but as we need them to be or desire them to be is called *fusion*. It is a seeing through the defences we erect to get our needs met.

For example, suppose I feel threatened and unloved when you disagree with me. I may believe that I need you to agree with me so that I can feel loved. Therefore, I let you know, both verbally and non-verbally, that you are lovable when you agree with me. I commend you for being "agreeable" (in both meanings of the term). You discover that when you agree with me, I seem to love you. Now we both feel loved. We have established a cozy collusion. In such a relationship where my disagreeing with you is fundamentally unacceptable, what will become of my sense of self?

Mirroring thus involves putting subtle and not-so-subtle pressure on the other to comply with our perceived needs of them.

Why, we might ask, do we let others put pressure on us to be as they desire? Why do we accommodate to their needs of us? Just as we said that the mirroring selves are not passive, similarly, the selves that are mirrored are not passive either. The second reason comes, then, from the side of the mirrored selves. We, too, have needs which become actively engaged in the mirroring process. In fact, we are invested at the level of basic survival.

Principle four states:

4. Each person needs to be loved and to matter.

As children, each of us needs our parents' love and approval. If not love and approval, at the very least, we need to matter. These needs are perceived not as a luxury but as a matter of survival. They are necessary for life.

It has been shown that the needs for emotional and physical closeness are basic biological needs on a par with physiological needs for food, water, and warmth. In the studies of French psychologist René Spitz[9], war-orphaned infants whose physiological needs were taken care of nevertheless sickened and even died because they were not adequately held and rocked by the beleaguered staff of the orphanage. This research revolutionized psychology. We can never again conceptualize human beings as purely physical creatures. We

9 Spitz, René: *The First Year of Life*, International Universities Press, New York, 1965.

are essentially beings in relationship.

Our needs for love and acceptance are primary. Narcissism arises out of the frustration of these basic needs. On the surface, narcissism presents as an intently engrossed self-absorption which seems to betoken extreme self-love. Narcissistic people are those of us who are so preoccupied with our own needs and wishes, it is as if we believed that nobody else could be as important as we are. Yet it is precisely because these needs were not adequately met in our earlier lives that they have become so pressing. It is because of the fear that they will never be met that they occupy such prominence in our lives, often to the exclusion of anyone else. What lies beneath this insistence on ourselves first and foremost is not self-love but self-doubt. We doubt we are worthy, that we are good enough to be loved.

What, we may ask, is the opposite of love? The answer is not hate but indifference. Love and hate are close bedfellows. They are intense ways of connecting, one positive, one negative. We can use rage to sustain connection. Sheer indifference severs connection. It is the experience of being flung into insignificance, nothingness, the void.

* * *

When, as a little girl at Camp Kawagama, I gazed out at the waves on Rocky Point, my longing was a longing for something different from what was given and permissible, a fantasy of something beyond, something I called "home". While it gave me loneliness and isolation, it also gave me consciousness. It was a kind of rude awakening. It was as if I implored the universe: "If this life I live is so deeply disappointing, what else is there?"

I could speculate that I became a philosopher, a romantic, and a rebel all in that moment's gaze. The "pain in the butt" designation carried with it the millstone of alienation as well as the heady freedom to be myself. Disappointment danced with daring. I was launched into the stormy pendulum swing of grandiosity and *inferiority depending on how I was feeling about being different. "If you can't beat 'em, join 'em" has as its logical counterpart "If you can't join 'em, beat 'em." I guess you could say I did both. I was skating on two skates headed in opposite directions. I strove for acceptability and then I repeatedly blew the acceptability game by taking some bold maverick stand. I could no more rest in the rebel role than I could in conformity. My sister put it succinctly when she said with a mixture of envy and disdain: "You were weird!"*

What earned me that designation? It was years before I ventured to pose that unmentionable question. My sins were trotted out like soiled underwear. "You ate yogurt! You liked classical music! You lived in the country! Remember that hayride you took us all on? Those artichokes you served us?" I was taken aback to discover that these were the visible signs that had marked me with the "disease" of unacceptability. She herself was a germ-free traditionalist. By then I had ventured far beyond the confines of the suburban Toronto Jewish housewife model by marrying outside the faith, studying Philosophy (a distinctly unfeminine subject), moving out west, and eventually becoming a single parent by choice.

Would my disease have progressed to such epidemic proportions had I realized that the cost of conformity might have been so easily averted by simply becoming a secret yogurt eater?

* * *

As we look into the mirror of our loved ones' faces, we discover that we are not, in some respects, what they would have us be. We see ourselves with parts lopped off (e.g. me minus my dissatisfaction or my neediness or my unconventionality). Most love is conditional: "I'll love you if. . . "

Consider this Laingian knot:[10]

The parent says (in effect):

"You bad girl. You are bad to talk back to me. You are bad

10 See Laing: R.D.: *Knots*, Penguin Books, Middlesex, England, 1970.

to be angry. To be angry is bad."

"I am good when I tell you you're bad. I'm angry when you're bad. But I'm not bad when I'm angry at your being bad because I am helping you to be good."

"If you are a good girl, then I will be happy. Good girls do not get angry and talk back to their parents. They are happy being good."

"If you are a good girl, then you'll be happy and I will be a good parent."

"Be my good girl and we'll both be happy and I will love you."

For the child, parents are like giants; they are bigger than life. They are like the blown up image of the wizard in *The Wizard of Oz*, with booming voices and huge faces and magical powers. Parents must know best.

There is a deep primal block to acknowledging serious flaws, limitations and faults in our parents.

Principle five states:

5. Each child wants to believe that his or her parents are okay.

Herein lies the idealization of the parent and our clinging, beyond all logic, to the lofty image we project. In the words of Stephen Levine:

How often are we like the battered child on the front page of the Los Angeles Times, being carried gently from the room by the compassionate matron, who reaches over the matron's shoulder shouting "Mama, Mama," to the woman in custody between the policemen on the other side of the room, arrested for burning the flesh and breaking the bones of this child? [11]

We cling to our abusers — or to our fantasy of them.

* * *

It is true that camp might not have been the abandonment trauma it was for me had it not inescapably illuminated the fact that my family were not as they pretended to be. At various time the unwelcome truth would surface against the backdrop of protestations to the contrary and we would all hasten back to the reassuring posture of being a loving family. In public at least.

I, more than anyone, tenaciously resisted registering what was going on – the pain behind the pretending. My sister said that in her fifties she was asked what love felt like and she suddenly realized she had no idea. Feeling was a disability in that world. Everyone went through the motions, mostly feeling empty and not knowing why.

It was a spawning ground for addictions. My sister equated having a good time with drinking too much, my father with eating too much. My mother popped an enormous array of prescription medications, and my brother walked around in his three hundred and fifty pound body insisting that he had a happy childhood. What I would now understand as emotional abuse was a daily way of relating.

It was a normal family on the surface, not dramatically different from the families around us. Nor was there any evil intention. Everyone was doing their best with what they knew. And everyone was hurting.

I was often told that I was the lucky child because I was born when my parents had money (enough money to send us to camp). But well before I was sent to camp, three years earlier, I was sent to school at age three and I had to stay in nursery school for three

---

11 Levine, Stephen: *Who Dies?*, Anchor Doubleday, New York, 1982, page 5.

years because I was too young for kindergarten. This was a very long time before preschools were popular so this was a very unusual thing. My mother's rather enigmatic explanation of why I was sent to school so early is that I wanted to go...??

There were several nannies in my first three years of life and then one who arrived when I was three and a half and stayed in my life for the next thirty-six years. My mother complained that she had to fight to be the one to give me my bath — and I had accepted this statement at face value without noticing any peculiarity. It was the nanny who was beside me when I had my afternoon naps, when I had whooping cough, when I got my first period and when I graduated from high school. It was the nanny who was there when my parents began wintering in Florida, first for two months, then for four months, then for six months of each year.

But I dearly wanted to believe it was all okay. One of our family sayings was: "When the chips are down, it's your family you can count on." They were there (except for my mother) when, at age twenty-three, I awoke from my coma, discovering I had not died, despite ingesting over fifty of my mother's Seconal tablets. "Enough to kill a cow!" the head nurse told me. So why didn't it kill me?

My brother, a lawyer by then, told me that I would be sent to jail if I did not enter the Psych ward because it was against the law to attempt suicide. I believed him and I was terrified of going to jail.

My sister said she thought I was "just trying to get attention" and that it was "a real bother" and just like me to be a pain in the butt.

My mother took to her bed and was very distraught. She never came to visit me. I called her from a pay phone in the hallway of the Psych ward a few days later. I remember her words exactly. She said: "How could you do this to me??"

Then she added: "I want you to know that if you ever try this again, you will take me with you. You will be responsible for my death as well as your own. I want you to remember that." I have always remembered.

Nothing more was said of it. Nobody asked me why I did it. I probably could not have answered them anyway.

* * *

This brings us to the most fundamental dilemma of the self: Given the choice between believing either that our parents are inherently mistaken, inadequate or bad or that we are, we inevitably choose the latter. It is better to believe that the fault lies in us than to acknowledge the flaws in our parents.

Where there is a conflict between what they say about us and what we feel, we assign the difficulty to our feelings. "It must be me; I'm bad; the problem is me." Even when we have no idea what we did wrong, we remain convinced that we are to blame. And we carry this conviction into adulthood.

How often have we seen our clients pull back in guilt, confusion and panic at the prospect of betraying their allegiance to their parents. The child in us confronts this inescapable crisis:

I need Mama.

Mama says (in effect): "Be who I say you should be."

Either Mama is right and good and if I do it, then (maybe) I will be loved.

Or Mama is wrong and bad and I am overwhelmed by fear, an innate primal fear that I will die, cast out into the void without my lifeline.

As a child I depend on the parent both physically and emotionally to survive. So what do I do? Inevitably the child crosses over, as it were, to the parental perspective and thereby abandons him or herself.

Hence, principle six states:

6. The child identifies with the parent and loses empathy with him or herself.

As this two-step from self to other has been described in depth by psychoanalyst Dr. Alice Miller[12], I refer to it as "the Alice Miller two-step." It has also been termed "identification with the aggressor"[13] in writings on abuse. At the deepest level, it constitutes the fundamental split in the self.

Because we believe we are bad and yet we need love, we have to change ourselves to get it, and our accommodation to the other's needs of us produces the false self.

If I am what you want me to be, I am compliant. If I am not what you want me to be, I am defiant.

Either I shove down my anger and become compliant (developing, for example, back problems, depression, or even in the extreme, cancer.). Or I refuse to suppress my anger and become defiant, acting as if I don't really need your love and approval at all. In the first case, I surrender to my need for you and my anger becomes disowned. In the second case, I identify with my anger and my neediness becomes disowned.

At their root, both compliance and defiance are responses to the threat of abandonment or collapse of the primary love bond. This threat is inevitable for all human beings because there will always be areas in which we feel that we did not get the love and attention we needed. Consequently, in those areas, we will develop defensive systems to compensate for what we feel we missed and to give us ways to survive.

12 See Miller, Alice: *The Drama of the Gifted Child*, Basic Books, New York, 1982; *For Your Own Good: Hidden Cruelty in Childrearing and the Roots of Violence*, The Noonday Press, New York. 1990; *The Untouched Key: Tracing Childhood Trauma in Creativity and Destructiveness*, Doubleday, New York, 1990; *Banished Knowledge: Facing Childhood Injuries*, Doubleday, New York, 1990; *Breaking Down the Wall of Silence: The Liberating Experience of Facing Painful Truth*, A Dutton Book, The Penguin Group, New York, 1991.
13 See, for example, Shengold, Leonard: *Soul Murder: The Effects of Childhood Abuse and Deprivation*, Fawcett Columbine, New York, 1989.

Both compliance and defiance have in common the fact that one's responses are determined by the other, rather than by the self. In the former case, your "yes" is my "yes"; in the latter, your "yes" is my "no." In neither case am I free to determine my own "yes" or "no". I abandon my autonomous self by referring my responses to the other and thereby acting from a false self. Contrast this false self with true autonomy aptly described by a poster I once saw as: "being whatever I want to be. . . even if my mother approves."

The false self is a self in reaction, an image or script written, not by me, but by the other. I look outside myself for my validation, responding to an external point of reference. The false self is, therefore, my accommodation to your demands of me.

Whatever does not fit this adapted self is relegated to the not-me, the part I call the shadow, the part that is disowned. The shadow, in this usage, is the part of me that is incompatible with my accommodation to your script for me. Hence the self becomes split into false self and shadow.

Principle seven states:

7. The false self is the child's accommodation to his or her parents' image. The shadow is the disowned, unacceptable part of the self.

In this way, the child's identification with the parent involves a loss of empathy with the split-off child or shadow part of the self. The split-off child becomes suppressed and repressed. It is the self we do not want to see. Inside of each of us is a child we have abandoned screaming to be loved.

* * *

It is curious that during that first summer at camp, almost all the youngest children, including myself, contracted chicken pox.

We were placed in quarantine in the infirmary and cautioned to stay away from all the other campers.

It was no fun at all being sick in that strange place without my mother. I recall waking up in the middle of the night in the pitch black realizing with panic and dismay that I had no idea how to find the john.

What was tremendous fun, though, was chasing other campers, all bigger than us, who ran from us yelping and squealing in all directions. What a surge of power that gave us! Having chicken pox became a weapon of extraordinary magnitude for a pock-marked bunch of five and six year olds who managed to sneak out of the infirmary. If desire for revenge can be understood as a natural response to having one's face rubbed in one's helplessness, this goes a long way toward explaining the enormous delight we took in this escapade.

To be marooned on an island, separated from my parents, and then quarantined in the infirmary, separated from the rest of the camp, still strikes me as a remarkably dramatic introduction to powerlessness.

Near the infirmary overlooking a swampy area by the shower house, a cage had been nailed up on a high pole. The atmosphere was dank and faintly macabre. I knew I was not supposed to be there. I was frightened but I had to see what was inside that cage.

It was wooden and had wire netting stretched across the open side that faced downhill toward the shower house. I did not like to have my back to the showers that were inexplicably menacing to me but it was the only way I could see inside the cage. I stood on tiptoes rather precariously. There was something black in there. Just as I peered in craning to see, it let out a piercing screech and scraped its huge black wings against the wire barricade.

Did the crow see me? I never knew. I was flying down the hill as fast as my legs would carry me. At the time, I thought it was, without doubt, the most evil thing I had ever seen. I did not understand that it had simply outgrown its cage and was screaming to be free. Nor did I see in this trapped, wretched creature someone who was rather like me.

*   *   *

In order to keep ourselves from seeing the shadow part of ourselves, we have to suppress or repress it - that is, make it unconscious. The function of the defense system is to keep the shadow suppressed. The guardian at the gate of the shadow is the Superego or what Robert Firestone[14] so aptly calls "the Voice." It represents the internalized parental injunctions that form our negative self-image, the inner critic that tyrannizes us from within with its system of shoulds and don'ts. It is, in effect, an inner self-policing system that compels us to follow the script of the false self and to deny conflicting aspects of ourselves which have been repressed in the shadow.

We now face a deeper level of psychological distress. The split in the self is an inherently untenable solution that generates inescapable pressure from within.

What has been forced into the unconscious by denial, gains power as a sort of subterranean or underground force. What has been disowned remains primitive, indirect, and unresolved. It creates an agitation in the self that presses for resolution. Thus, the more the shadow is suppressed, the more it will be acted out.

The implications of this inner pressure will be felt on two levels: First, what is unconscious in one generation will be acted out in the next. Second, what is unconscious in one's own past will be acted out in the present.

Due to the force of the shadow, the past dogs us. It can never be shucked off and discarded for good. The shadow drags the repressed aspects of the self into the present and forces us to face them again and again. We will inevitably reenact our family of origin issues in our relationships with significant others, including bosses, employees, spouses and children.

Intimate love relationships are particularly hard hit. We

14 Firestone, Robert: *The Fantasy Bond*, Human Sciences Press, New York, 1987, Ch. 6.

inevitably project our unfinished business with our parents on to our partners. The postures of compliance and defiance we spoke of earlier will appear as conflict phobias and control battles in the marital sphere. Because of the inevitability of this type of projection, it is difficult to know, as Virginia Satir used to say, "mit whom we are having the pleasure."[15]

* * *

It has been said that one can look at a person's life from the perspective that it has all been lived emotionally in one key place[16]. Camp Kawagama would be that place for me. My life could be portrayed like the TV series "The Prisoner" as a succession of bold and daring attempts to escape the island and be free. (I always liked that series.) And I was always trying to escape the expectations that imprisoned me.

"Tune in tomorrow for her third and final daring attempt to leave Toronto. Watch reruns of her bold forays out of the affluent Jewish ghetto that was Forest Hill" (honestly, as I wrote the manuscript, I made a typo and typed Forest Hell!) Remember that I was "a nice Jewish girl" who was supposed to marry at 19, settle down in Toronto with a nice Jewish doctor or lawyer and have babies. University education was considered a waste of time for a girl like me.

Yet my first job was at a YMCA day camp. I did not marry until I was 26 and my first husband was an Irish Catholic. I did not have babies until I was close to 40 and had moved out to the west coast of Canada, as far from Toronto as I could get. I got two Masters degrees and a Doctorate. Perhaps all that education warped my mind. I fell in love with an English Protestant atheist (although he may have changed his mind about God later) and ended up a single parent alone and in debt. The episodes line up all too readily.

---

15 For Satir's views on projection in marital and family relationships see, for example, Satir, Virginia: *Conjoint Family Therapy*, Science & Behavior Books, Palo Alto, 1967, and *Peoplemaking*, Science and Behavior Books, Palo Alto, 1972.
16 Comment made by Arnold Mindell in a Process workshop entitled "Inner Work - World Work" offered in Vancouver, B.C., February 19-21, 1993

It would be no surprise to reenactment theorists that even forty-five years later, I was longing for a beloved I could not see and could not even telephone. And into the next generation, my son was longing for the man he called his dad, who refused to see him and would not return his calls.

As I write, I have to ask myself: am I still trying to write my way out of camp?

* * *

With the split of the self and the denial of the shadow, we enter the realm of distortion of both self and other. We have seen that the child idealizes the parent and suppresses information that would acknowledge basic faults, limitations and flaws in the parent. To this extent, we deny the shadow in the parent.

At the same time, we deny the shadow in ourselves as we assume images that are either inflated, pretending we are better than we are, or deflated, pretending we are worse. In fact, however, the one does not exist without the other. If our conscious stance is superiority, our feelings of inadequacy will be present on the unconscious level. If we present as inferior, our pretensions to grandeur will be hidden in our perfectionistic expectations of ourselves. Grandiosity implies inferiority and vice versa. Both are rejections of the self as it is. In his book, *Compassion and Self-Hate*, Theodore Isaac Rubin says:

> Any distortion of self, either in degradation or idealization, must be viewed as rejection of actual self and is therefore self-hating. Thus, exaggerated opinions as to one's abilities are no more, no less, self-hating. Rejection of reality as regards self, whatever form that distortion takes, always makes for destructive repercussions in terms of actual self. [17]

It follows, then, that grandiosity and inferiority rest on the same footing. They are both instances of rejection of the self

---

17 Rubin, Theodore Isaac: *Compassion and Self-Hate: An Alternative to Despair,* Collier Books, New York, 1975, page 9.

as it is, which is the essence of self-hate.

Principle eight is:

8. Self-hate is the rejection of the self as it is. It includes both poles of narcissism - grandiosity and inferiority.

The corollary of the rejection of the self as it is, (which is self-hate) is the rejection of the other as they are - which is fusion, as we saw earlier. Fusion is the perception of the other through the filter of our needs and desires and the resulting demand that they be as we want them to be. In order to justify ourselves in this demand, we see ourselves as entitled or as acting within our rights. In so doing, we implicitly perceive the other as within the domain of our will. We treat them as if they were part of us like they are the tail and we are the dog, as one of my teachers, Andrew Feldmar, used to say. Fusion is based on the perception of the other as an extension of the self and therefore as within the boundaries of one's right to exert pressure and exercise control. We say: this is my child, my wife, my husband. We puff up with self-righteousness because we only acted, we insist, for their own good. Or we are appalled at a family member's behavior because we worry about what people will think of us. Fusion is, therefore, a perception of the other as within the boundaries of one's own self.

Principle nine states:

9. Fusion is the failure to perceive the other as a separate self. It is, therefore, a boundary violation.

Because we fail to see the other as a separate self, we try to control them. Because we believe that we need them to be certain ways in order for us to survive, we try to change them. Because we feel justified in placing our demands on the other, we try to force them to be as we wish. Control, coercion, pressure, and force are all abusive. It follows, then, that fusion forms the ground for abuse in relationships.

In a parallel way, we also reject our own selves as we are. We try to control ourselves, change ourselves, force ourselves to be as we think we should be. The attempt to exert control, coercion, pressure, and force on the self are all self-abusive.

Therefore, principle ten states:

10. Fusion leads to abuse of the other; self-hate leads to abuse of the self.

In both cases, refusal to accept the truth of who we are leads to distortion, denial and abuse.

*   *   *

Almost fifty years later, I was at another "rocky point" in my life when my mate walked out a week after we had just purchased a house together. I was in a frenzy of emotional and financial distress as I watched the reenactment of my abandonment pattern unfold again.

My sister offered help and then withdrew the offer, likely prompted by my brother who immediately shot out: "I'm not going to help you!" I resisted pointing out that I had not asked him for help.

My mother called to see how I was doing.

"Do you want the official press report or do you want the truth?" I asked her.

Staunchly she replied: "You don't have to ice the cake for me!"

"Well, then, terrible," I admitted.

*"I don't tell you **my** troubles," she said.*

*   *   *

We now have the full cycle of abuse as it operates from

generation to generation, the sins of the fathers being visited upon the sons. This cycle is summarized in Diagram A. It shows that, as we idealize our parents and deny their shadow parts, we cross over to the parent perspective and lose empathy with ourselves. This is the Alice Miller two-step. The rejected or disowned self becomes repressed and we are unable to empathize with any manifestations of this shadow in others or in ourselves.

To the extent that we suppress the shadow in ourselves, we will be unable to recognize the abusive nature of our dealings with others. The traits that are most disowned in ourselves will be the traits that we find most reprehensible in other people. It is chilling, indeed, to realize that that which we most hate in the other is a mirror of our own disowned selves.

Denial of the shadow is generated by the wish to ensure our acceptability by becoming what we believe the other wants us to be. It contains within it the reciprocal demand for the other to be as we want them to be. In this fusion of self and other, we enter the domain of manipulation, power and control. We abuse and we are abused. As a final step, we then deny this abuse with a cruel sleight of hand: we call it love.

*　*　*

DIAGRAM A	
Narcissistic Cycle	
PARENT	CHILD
Denies shadow of his/her parent	Denies shadow of own parent
Identifies with parent	Identifies with own parent
Loses empathy with self	Loses empathy with self
Denies own shadow	Denies own shadow
Loses empathy with other	Loses empathy with others

Abuse Cycle

Therefore, we need enough ego strength – through
bonding – to see ourselves as abused and abusive, damaged
and damaging

* * *

*Voices crowd for hearing. Voices of anger, sadness, protest,
and righteous indignation. These are all victim voices. We are all
victims of victims.*

*There I was at a meditation retreat with Ram Dass in the
woods in Oregon. The reenactment was raging. The cabin I had
reserved several months before turned out not to exist. My teacher/
colleague/ friend had turned against me and I felt unwelcome in
her van. It was a betrayal scene much like the one with my sister
at camp. I found myself stuck in line at the john, living out in
excruciating anguish the label, "pain in the butt." It was a block that
seemed to be immoveable and it hurt. As the line for the toilet kept*

growing, I could neither go, nor could I leave. The pain was real, the frustration was legitimate, the sadness was heart-wrenching. At the same time, I had to chuckle. It was beyond pathetic. It was ridiculous.

How many times would I play out the same scene? When would I stop being shocked and devastated by other people's cruelty? It was up to me, wasn't i? – to care for this hurt child? I began to care for myself in the nurturing way I had taught so well to others. I began to parent the child inside of me.

It was a very diffident, distrustful and hurt child that I learned to parent that week, a child beset by message after message of abandonment and rejection. I listened to the old scripts, so worn and familiar, with a new detachment. I walked in the ancient forest amid trees that had stood there for centuries. They had never even heard of Camp Kawagama. And if I had not written this story, neither would you.

*   *   *

We have traced the process of splitting in the self from the first recognition of a boundary between self and other through the crossover to identification with the other and disavowal of the self. We are left fractured into false self and shadow, yearning to be loved.

In the next section, we will explore in depth how this yearning is twisted and corrupted in the domain of emotional abuse.

Part Two

Emotional Abuse:
Breaking the Spell

. . . and then the day came
    when the risk to remain tight in a bud
        was more painful than the risk it took to blossom.

                                        Anais Nin

All abuse is soul-shattering, but emotional abuse has its own peculiar treachery in that it is all-pervasive and yet so subtle and difficult to detect. Consequently, as victims, we may suffer the paralyzing effects of abuse while being unable to identify that abuse has occurred.

Physical abuse creates bruises and broken bones which can be seen, X-rayed, and treated by medical technology. Thus we have no difficulty in recognizing physical abuse. Yet all physical abuse has emotional abuse as a component.

Sexual abuse has been more difficult to acknowledge than physical abuse although we are now waking up to the extent and trauma of sexual abuse. Yet all sexual abuse has emotional abuse as a component.

Beyond both of these exists the huge domain of emotional abuse involving neither physical nor sexual abuse. Its impact, though invisible, is no less widespread and pernicious. Why something so universal can nevertheless escape our notice is that emotional abuse has largely been treated as "the way life is" and not seen as abuse at all.

Among everyday examples of abuse, I include:

belittling, teasing, put-downs, bullying, mocking, ridiculing, nagging, name-calling, scapegoating, lying about someone or to someone, misrepresenting, deceiving, invalidating, constant criticism, character assassination, verbal assault, threatening, intimidating, emotional blackmail, ignoring, neglecting, excluding, rejecting, withholding, objectifying, abandoning, deserting, betraying, and undermining another's sense of self.

Anything familiar here? The list could go on. This is ordinary life, the domain of the normal family: garden-variety domestic squabbles, sibling rivalry, and marital strife. This is the world of "The Simpsons," of "Married with Children", and of "Southpark." It's funny, isn't it?

To characterize these all-too-common and homey

examples of everyday life as emotional abuse will most likely be regarded as hystrionic and grossly exaggerated. At the very least, it will be viewed as an overreaction. This minimizing type of response to the identification of emotional abuse is, regrettably, the most frequent and predictable one. Because we have grown accustomed to emotional abuse as a constant presence in our lives, it is virtually invisible to us. It is as obvious as the air around us and as difficult to see.

Symptoms arise in every dimension of our being – the physical, emotional, cognitive, behavioral and interpersonal. First, on the physical level: we often get sick, not in a life-threatening way, but in a subclinical constellation of nagging signs indicating that our bodies are making a protest. Symptoms such as headaches, sinus infections, stomach aches, diarrhea, gas pains, constipation, nausea, dizziness, fatigue, muscle and joint pain, flu–like symptoms – in other words, the most common complaints seen by the medical profession – may all be physical manifestations of an underlying malaise.

According to Arnold Mindell, founder of Process Therapy, the damage wrought by emotional abuse will be experienced primarily in the region from the chest to the face. [18] In my experience, it most frequently centers in the throat. Survivors of emotional abuse typically experience sore throats, frequent dryness, hoarse or high squeaky voices, chronic coughing, wheezing, and throat infections. The throat is choked off. This is an expression of our deep-seated difficulty in speaking out.

* * *

When I was little, I used to awaken with what I call a "cramp" in my throat. I couldn't breathe and as I went to scream "Mama", no sound would come out. It was as though there was a hand around my neck choking me and I had no voice.

It is true that I accepted my fate without much protest. Why did

18 Mindell, Arnold, comment in a Process workshop entitled "Inner Work - World Work", Vancouver, February 1993.

I acquiesce so easily? Where was my voice back then? I wonder to myself looking back: why didn't I stubbornly persist in phoning my mother night after night until she heard me? Or refuse to participate in camp activities? Or repeat over and over like a recording that would not stop that I wanted to go home; I just wanted to go home. What if I had called her bluff and flatly refused to go to camp each and every summer? What if I had told her just how wretchedly unhappy I was? Why was it never an option to do or say anything like that?

*I remember a talk I had with my sister that first summer at camp – or, more aptly, it was a talk she had with me. She was twelve and I was five. We were standing at the "Y" where the two paths to our cabins diverged and went off in opposite directions. This conversation was memorable because she had not talked to me for several weeks since I was blackballed from going to her cabin. She warned me menacingly that I was not under any circumstances to complain or say anything negative about camp to our parents on Visitors' Day. The details of her threat are lost but the message was loud and clear. I held it in my throat for years. I **had to shut up and take it.** For most of my childhood there was a hand clamped over my mouth that silenced me.*

Once, many years later, I developed laryngitis, an obviously difficult condition for a psychotherapist whose voice is the tool of her trade. It was just after my mate was accused by his ex-wife of abusing their youngest daughter. I didn't realize the two events were connected until, in a hypnotherapy session, I tracked the origin of the symptom back to wanting to scream and what came up was his ex-wife's face. Convinced of the malevolence behind this accusation, I was choked with rage.

I recognize this as a long- familiar feeling. I wonder if, like myself, many women have a silent scream they have been screaming their whole lives.

In my Gestalt therapy training, I worked on my voice over and over, disgruntledly, until I could find the energy and sound for that voice.

In the women's movement, I fought for my voice as a woman – for the right to be listened to and, with other women, for the right to speak out with pride in our common voice.

In my writing now, I struggle to find in the space between pretensions to grandeur and fears of worthlessness the clear sound of my own voice.

I think the metaphor of the voice is particularly poignant for female survivors.

* * *

Second, on the emotional level, one might say that symptoms of emotional abuse are literally walking into our therapy offices every hour of every day. By far the most familiar symptoms would be depression, anxiety and low self-esteem in their multi-faceted variations. We witness how this triad plays out in the constant self-denigration and self-destructive patterns, the feelings of being worthless and unacceptable, the fears of being stupid and incompetent, the feeling of being watched and judged incessantly, the desire to hide, the inner shaking, and the feeling that at any moment we are about to be hurt.

In writing my first paper on emotional abuse, I watched my feelings run the gamut from depression to anxiety to obsession with conflicting messages such as:

"Why did I ever agree to give a paper on this topic? What on earth was I thinking?"
to:
"You should have done this ages ago! What took you so long??"
to:
"How can I get myself out of this nightmare?"
to:
"How can you even *think* of getting out?"
and from:

"There is too much to say on this topic! I can't say anything of value in thirty minutes! I'd need at least two days!"
to:
"You have nothing to say on this topic. How could you imagine you have something valuable to contribute? Doesn't everybody already know what you are about to say?"

This swing from having so much of importance to say to having nothing of importance to say is the swing described in the Object Relations literature as the movement from grandiosity to inferiority, the essence of the narcissistic bind. It is described by John Bradshaw[19], a spokesman for Adult Children of Alcoholics, as a movement from superhuman to subhuman expectations, from trying to be more than we are to seeing ourselves as less.

In its logical structure, it exemplifies what I describe as a "teeter-totter" or a "pendulum" because it involves a dynamic balancing of opposites in such a way that, even though one may be conscious and the other unconscious, both are always present and of equal force.

For example, a depressed client complained one day that she felt like the worst person in the universe. Without facetiousness, I asked her: "What makes you so important?" Behind her overwhelming feeling of inferiority lurked the grandiose expectations she had of herself. In the light of these inflated expectations, she could only view herself with grave disappointment. Such an example illustrates in an extreme the Gestalt dictum: "every complaint is a brag."

The teeter-totter theory enables us to resist the easy assumption that what is apparent on the surface is all there is. It moves us to search deeper for the concealed opposite of that which is obvious. Thus we discover that compliance hides its opposite - defiance – in the form of anger turning inward against the self (as in depression) or leaking out sideways (as

---

19 Bradshaw, John: *Healing the Shame That Binds You*, Health Communications, Deerfield Beach, Florida, 1988.

in passive aggression) or being acted out in self-destructive sabotage. By the same reasoning, defiance hides its opposite - compliance – in the form of excessive demands on the other coming from neediness and an inability to let go.

* * *

I sucked my thumb until I was fourteen years old. Frankly, I didn't see any reason to give it up. As far as I was concerned, my thumb did an excellent job of soothing me. Perhaps as a clinician, I would be expected to show concern about this fact but, as an advocate for the child, I think it was a remarkably effective strategy. My thumb was there with unquestionable reliability, close at hand (so to speak) and constantly accessible. It never let me down.

Unfortunately, there was heavy pressure from my family to give it up. Likely out of fear of huge orthodontist bills, my parents and the dentist conspired to invent an alarming tale. They told me that my thumb would shrink from all the sucking and would eventually wither away. I believed them. While I was not smart enough as a child to see through this hoax, I was smart enough to figure out that I'd just keep on sucking until my thumb started to shrink.

I used to measure it carefully every night. I'd line up the creases in my two wrists and check one thumb against the other. If you've never tried this exercise, you might not realize just how difficult it is to get the wrist creases to line up exactly. How many times I gasped in horror as the right thumb measured smaller than the left! Then, with held breath, I'd line them up again ever so carefully.

This was one drama in my life that always had a happy ending: my thumb proved to be unshrinkable after all.

* * *

Third, the cognitive symptoms of abuse that are most prevalent include lack of concentration, memory impairment, confusion and distractibility. All too frequently we might find ourselves crossing a room only to realize we have no idea what we were going for. We may suddenly have an aphasic block for perfectly ordinary words or be unable to recall a name as familiar as our own. At times we may wonder about early senility when it is in fact the impact of abuse that is interfering with our normal functioning in these disturbing ways.

Our capacity for rigorous logical reasoning may definitely be adversely affected. A familiar example of this sort of malfunction in reasoning occurs when we compartmentalize information in such a way that strikingly obvious conclusions fail to be drawn. It is as if we hold "two" in one bin and "two" in another, yet the mind is unable to combine them, hold them simultaneously, and move to the obvious "four."

As a case in point: my mate made a promise to me that carried serious implications for my life. I was well aware that he had broken most of his promises up to that time. The obvious conclusion which should have been drawn (and was *not* drawn) by me was: he might - in fact he probably will - break this promise too. He did. And was I shocked! Why? Because this time, I thought, would be *different!*

This bizarre reasoning may be categorized as a *thought impairment*. It is akin to the "insanity" defined by Alcoholics Anonymous as: continuing to act in a manner which has, in the past, always produced a certain effect, believing that *next time*, it will produce a different, even opposite, one.

As well as afflicting alcoholics and lovers, such blatant illogicality is conspicuous in victims of abuse, particularly battered wives, and can be extremely frustrating both for the victims and for those working with them. Perhaps we can be more compassionate if we recall that this type of impairment is a defensive maneuver driven by the unconscious mind and not mere willfulness or stubbornness on their part.

* * *

Defeated in the dental psychology realm, my parents decided to tie a leather armband around the elbow joint on my right (thumb-sucking) arm. The idea was to prevent me from being able to bend my arm and raise my thumb to my mouth. I discovered that, if I tried and tried, straining with all my might against the leather, I could just touch the tip of my thumb to my lips.

When I bragged about this feat of strength and agility, they didn't believe me so I offered to give a public demonstration in the living room. Everyone assembled and I felt very important. I gave a masterful exhibition of determined defiance for which I was rewarded with my favorite maraschino cherry chocolate. Although it must have been apparent that the band still made sucking my thumb impossible, thankfully that was the end of the leather armband torture.

Presumably, it was my fear of ridicule by my peers that finally compelled me to give up thumb-sucking at age fourteen. Three years later, I had become a confirmed cigarette smoker, inhaling one to two packs a day. I continued this habit for the next seventeen years. When I finally quit smoking, I developed a weight problem for the first time in my life. This problem has remained with me ever since. In retrospect, I think I'd have to say I would been better off to keep on sucking my thumb.

Years later, I found myself grappling with love addiction, perhaps the most agonizing addiction of them all. I was consumed by longing for the man I still loved who had left. I was inconsolable, not unlike a child who has lost her pacifier and is utterly bereft. All at once I had the image of this man as a life-sized soother who had walked away. This seemed a rather amusing metaphor until I thought about MY THUMB. Suddenly it was no laughing matter.

*A thumb to a devoted thumb-sucker is a matter of serious concern. It has a distinctive taste and taste and texture that feels "just right" and is unique and irreplaceable. Even the thumb on the other hand would simply not be the same. The methodology of thumb-sucking is to prime the thumb a little until it tastes right and then work it into the position that feels right. Thumb-sucking is an exacting art. One certainly would not accept some other person's thumb as a replacement. It is that particular thumb we want – **our*** *very own* thumb – *just as a broken-hearted lover is not consoled by the promise of other potential partners when the one she loves has gone away.*

My thumb afforded me a novel appreciation of love addiction from both sides of the relationship. The unbearable longing of the lover is literally experienced as losing a part of oneself. It is like suffering an amputation that will not heal. Imagine if my thumb had been lopped off! It would have been the annihilation of the primary source of comfort in my universe.

On the other hand, imagine the plight of the loved one going through life being someone else's thumb!

* * *

Fourth, behavioral symptoms run the gamut of addictive and self-defeating behavior patterns that threaten our success in relationships, in our personal projects and career goals. We have a choice of many cunning and elaborate ways to sabotage ourselves.

A case in point is the first paper I wrote on emotional abuse. Ordinarily at the obsessive compulsive end of the continuum, this paper was an exception to the rule. I never did get the paper written by the publication deadline for the conference although I did manage to deliver it on time. I noticed myself employing several self-sabotaging strategies including indecisiveness, procrastination, compulsive eating, spacing out, and fantasizing. As the date loomed closer, instead of writing as I should have been, I found myself staring into space eating an O'Henry bar or hanging on the refrigerator door peering into the lit interior, searching for the right word.

When not thinking about food, I'd be thinking about that certain man. Sleeping became difficult in either case. I dreamt I got up to lecture in front of a room full of people and could not remember what I was supposed to lecture on (regrettably, a recurring dream.) As the deadline for the paper got closer,

I would have sworn my children got more difficult. (It was them, of course, not me.)

What better way to ground the theory of emotional abuse I was writing about than to experience some characteristic symptoms in the writing.

In the interpersonal sphere, emotional abuse wreaks havoc on our relationships. In my practice I work with people in conflict with each other and also in conflict with themselves. In fact, the conflict one has with the other is often a mirror of the conflict within oneself.

Essentially, difficulties in relationships are the working out of the dynamics of fusion in which we try to force both ourselves and others to be as we insist. When we reject the shadow or disowned parts of ourselves and our significant others, we are plunged into the triad of depression, anxiety, and low self-esteem that was mentioned above. In these painful states of being, we are seriously inhibited in maintaining interpersonal contact and developing intimacy in relationships.

For example, the difficulty that victims of abuse commonly experience in focusing and sustaining eye contact is due to the intrusion of dissociative and trancelike states evidenced by their fluttering eyelids, their rapid blinking, their staring vacantly ahead, and their looking without seeing. Since contact with others in the past has proved to be so perilous, they are understandably reluctant to face the perils again.

One popular alternative is to escape into addictions to dull the yearning and numb the pain. Our culture's all-consuming absorption in sex and romance, smoking, drinking and drugs, TV and shopping, overeating, over-achieving and over-work are all indicators of the same deep-seated discontent.

The conclusion we are drawn to is that the concerns we meet in therapy, the relationship problems, fears and phobias, depression, low self-esteem, and various addictions, are all symptoms of emotional abuse. Hence psychotherapy is, in essence, the treatment of emotional abuse.

While the symptoms of abuse are all around us and affect every facet of our being –physical, emotional, behavioral and interpersonal – we remain oblivious, as if we were asleep. It is only by awakening from our trance-like spell that we will begin to see that what is normal may be abusive and that symptoms may be calls to healing.

* * *

My need for solace becomes understandable when I bring to awareness my inner map of that supposed place of sanctity – my bedroom. An ordinary observer would have seen twin pine beds set side by side with a matching pine dresser in the room I shared with my sister. Beside her bed was the window and beside my bed was the clothes closet. Frilly curtains framed the window and the shelf beside it held our collection of dolls and stuffed animals. Who would have suspected that beneath this perfectly ordinary and innocent exterior lurked the menacing inner world of my childhood.

In the closet lived the boogie man, an undefined shadowy figure who lurked in the dark corners behind the hanging clothes. He had some vague association with dirt and snot, the memory of which still fills me with revulsion. When I lay in my bed, I knew he was crouching there, on my left, way back in the blackness, waiting. I always insisted that the closet door be closed.

On my right, at the window, the hideous face of the wicked witch of the west would appear, suddenly and without warning, with her crooked beaked nose, her beady eyes, and her sinister cackle. By some strange quirk of perception, the room would become elongated and her image transformed into silhouette. I've never figured out how this distortion occurred, but I know that it was terrifying.

As if these horrors on either side of me were not enough, my sister convinced me that in the space between our beds dwelt the crocodiles – green slithering creatures who were always hungry. Sometimes in the middle of the night when the fear overtook me, I would jump the gauntlet from my bed to hers, making sure to jump as high as I possibly could so that the crocodiles did not snap at my toes. With this enormous leap in the air, I must have landed on top of her with quite a thud. But she never complained too much and I never questioned the veracity of her stories. Gratefully, I would crawl into her bed and huddle at the very edge of the mattress with my leg gripped over the far side. As long as I didn't move too much or touch her, I was allowed to stay. Clinging to the edge of her bed, with the hall light shining in my eyes, was the closest I came to a feeling of safety in those days.

Years later, when my youngest son developed night fears, I made up the words for him that that frightened little girl would have wished to hear.

> "Mommy magic all around
> Keep this little child safe and sound.
> No bad things of any sort,
> Even Nukies,* bad thoughts or bad dreams
> Can come **anywhere** near here.

Then I drew a line with my foot across the threshold of his bedroom granting it immunity from danger.

He never sucked his thumb.

* * *

To get to the root of why emotional abuse is so pervasive and at the same time so deeply denied, we need to understand the logic of abuse and the way it is perpetuated.

The preconditions for abuse have already been explicated in Part One. Let us review our conclusions.

You will recall that the self gains its self-image through mirroring by the other. This mirroring is intrinsically affected by the needs that both self and other bring into their interaction. To the extent that I need you to love and approve of me, I will be receptive to your picture of me and motivated to shape myself in response to it. Thus arises the false self.

---

* Extraterrestrial creatures with dripping noses and misshapen heads in a children's movie that frightened him.

If you are a significant other, I will be inclined to see myself and to treat myself in accordance with the way you see me and treat me. My vulnerability to your mirroring of me joins forces with your tendency to exert pressure on me to meet your needs. Those reactions I have which are incompatible with your image of me will be repressed and thereafter acted out unconsciously in my dealings with you. Thus arises the shadow.

At the same time and in a parallel way, you are being influenced by my mirroring of you and you possess a reservoir of repressed reactions which are acted out in your responses to me. We begin to see how self and other participate in a reciprocal mirroring and shaping process which engages two different levels of functioning - the conscious and the unconscious, the false self and the shadow.

Our denial of the shadow in the other causes us to idealize them and repress our own truth. Thus we adopt the victim role.

The denial of the shadow in the self causes us to invalidate the negative responses of the other and idealize ourselves. Thus we adopt the abuser role.

It is crucial to emphasize that both roles are necessary and mutually dependent. We cannot have one without the other. Emotional abuse is a dynamic relationship between abuser and abused in which both are essential and play their part. I call it a "dance." This term suggests movement and the synchronized rhythm of two participants, each necessary, active and involved. It takes, we might say, "two to tango." In the victim/abuser dance, both abuser and abused are in trance - that is, they move in and out of dissociative states whose function it is to deny the abusive nature of their relationship and their mutual dependence on it.

The abuser is characterized by his or her inability to take in feedback. That is, in response to the protests or cries of pain of the victim, the abuser typically responds with: "Don't be such a cry-baby!" "You make such a fuss over everything!" "You think *that* hurts? Try *this!*" "There you go with your poor-me whining again!" The abuser's response is essentially denial and invalidation.

We may be greatly chagrined to discover that, when we respond to the identification of abuse with denial and invalidation, we are, in effect, slipping into the abuser role.

* * *

The first time I was to publicly present my theory of therapy – not the Gestalt theory or Virginia Satir's theory or anyone else's theory as I had done before – but my own theory, I felt rather anxious and vulnerable. I guess you could say I was a nervous wreck. My self-esteem was hanging by a thread and the presentation was coming up fast.

After much bashing and thrashing about, I had finally ground out a first draft. Nervously, I asked my mate if he would be interested in hearing it. (He was a psychologist after all.)

"Sure," he said. "Pass me the newspaper."

"What do you need the newspaper for when I'm about to read you my paper?" I inquired ingenuously.

"I can read the newspaper and listen to you at the same time," he said.

This incident recalls the sinking feeling I had when I sent my mother a good rope-style necklace I had selected for her birthday. I had seen an elegant colleague wearing one like it and I thought it would look great on my Mom. A few weeks later, it came back in the mail with a note of explanation. "You must have liked this" she said, "or you would not have bought it so I'm sending it back to you."

My mate said he didn't mean any offense and I'm sure my mother didn't either.

* * *

We have seen that as victims we "cross over" in the Alice

Miller two-step and end up on the other side. We become identified with caregivers who reproach and criticize. In this crossing over, we lose connection with our own voice, our point of reference from within. As a consequence, we find it hard to stand behind ourselves or hold a solid point of view. Our sense of self is fragile and shot through with fear. The voice that now inhabits us is no longer our own.

In each new crisis, we will feel shattered as if our whole world just exploded or the bottom fell out. In the encounter with others, we get lost in self-doubt and self-rebuke. We can't contain ourselves. Our boundaries are like Swiss cheese. What world we thought we had is ripped open, exposing the meager threads that were holding it together. We want to scream and cry and run away, but there is nowhere to hide. We are catapulted into blackness, into fear and confusion. We are locked in what feels like another space, another time, not knowing where we are. Just that the pain of it is familiar, like a very old wound.

This experience has been described by Almaas as "falling into a black hole" or, simply, "a hole." [20] The language of this description is purposely dramatic. The language of emotional drama and intensity must be used if we are to accurately capture the phenomenology of this experience, for what is being described here is *trauma*. Not the universally recognized traumas of major proportions such as beatings, murders and rape. These are the little traumas that pass unnoticed and unmentioned, the barely visible traumas of every day. To expose the underlying dynamic of this type of mundane experience is like taking an X-ray of emotional abuse.

It is as if a pin were stuck in the false self and the balloon suddenly burst. We are hurled back into the original experience of splitting that was repressed in childhood. We feel the pain, the loss, the rage. But we also feel the child's terror that to let in this experience would mean to face the unthinkable truth-

---

[20] cf. Almaas, A.H.: *Diamond Heart Book One*, Chapter Two, "The Theory of Holes", Diamond Books, Almaas Publications, Berkeley, 1987.

that those we love are hurting us and abusing us without reason or remorse.

Hastily the Superego leaps in to disarm this terror by challenging the validity of the experience and turning it against the self. "You bad girl. . . "Mommy would never..." "How could you think that . . " "You are so unfair, selfish, foolish, mean". "It is you who are to blame." The child contracts against the experience, feeling guilty and ashamed, while the truth creeps away into the background behind the smoke screen of our self-hate.

Not until the victim learns to dis-identify from the attacks of the Superego will the child's repressed feelings and perceptions be recognized and reowned. Until then, they will surface and be repressed, over and over again, in a continuous recycling process. Until then, we cannot stand behind ourselves or firmly occupy our own point of view. There is no spaciousness inside us, no place to take a stand. We are surrounded by witches, crocodiles and boogie men, with no "room of our own."[21]

*   *   *

It is odd that I have mentioned nothing about my brother. You might conclude from this omission that he was relatively unimportant or marginal in my life. The truth is quite the opposite. He was my idol and, in some ways, the most deep-seated influence on me. Perhaps this is why I find it such a struggle not to protect him.

By contrast, my sister, being seven years my senior, almost disappeared into the next generation. This age difference, already substantial, was exacerbated by the fact that when she was sixteen, she went to live at my aunt's following a fight with my father and she stayed there for more than a year. Shortly after her return home, she got engaged to be married and had moved out again within a year. She always claimed that the reason she got married was so that she could "buy all the lamb chops she wanted" but

21 cf. Woolf, Virginia: *A Room of One's Own*, Flamingo, An Imprint of Harper Collins Publishers, Hammersmith, London, 1984.

the income of a newly married eighteen-year-old couple made the purchase of lamb chops prohibitive. The real reason was simple: she wanted to get out of the house.

Her absence cleared an open path to my brother, two years her junior, who had never paid any attention to me while she was there. I gladly scooped up the opportunity. At nine years old, I was grateful for any attention I could get. And I mean **any**. I was like a little puppy dog jumping excitedly if he so much as turned my way and perpetually eager to come racing back with ears flapping and tail wagging in spite of being shunned. For years, I helped him study material that was meaningless to me – from Latin to French to taxation law. I acted as his decoy when he practiced basketball in the basement and often bashed me into the side walls. Though I huffed and puffed trying to grab that ball, he never let me get it away from him. After all, I was five years younger, a good deal smaller, and a **girl**.

He never let me forget my one-down position. He would grumble disdainfully about all the marbles I repeatedly lost at public school. Of course, **he** was a winner. Periodically, he would sail down gallantly, if somewhat contemptuously, from high school and win them all back for me. My knight in shining armor! I was so proud of him and so ashamed of me. He got first-class grades in school without even trying, whereas I worked assiduously to get my A's. It was a difference he was forever pointing out to me. Yet try as I might, I could never catch up. I was never smart enough or strong enough to compete.

We used to wrestle every Sunday morning because this was something he always liked to do. The memory of our wrestling on his double bed more than forty years ago is still excruciatingly fresh for me. In my recollection, I was almost always pinned down flat. He would tease me with little opportunities to break free. I'd taste the hopefulness when suddenly a leg sprang loose and I would leap to overpower him. To no avail. I was instantly subdued. His favorite was the position he called "the banana split" (I never got the reference back then) in which he held me down between his *legs, gloating at my immobility. He was triumphant; I was trapped and defeated. Not to mention, to my enduring embarrassment, incurably innocent and naïve.*

What an introduction to power and domination! He never let me win. We would carry on until, inevitably, he hurt me and I had to call for help to make him stop. Every Sunday morning when they rescued me, they'd say: "Why do you play with him? You know you always end up in tears."

How could I explain that I was desperate for the contact? How could I say this was my big brother whom I adored? How could I admit to myself or anyone else that he enjoyed hurting me? I was no better at it forty years later when this pattern was reenacted with my mate. I did not know about the victim/abuser dance in those days.

* * *

When we occupy the victim position, we take on any or all of the following three stances:

(1) We believe that we are over-reacting and thereby deny our own pain. This is explicit identification with the abuser.

(2) We believe we deserve what is happening to us or have brought it on ourselves and are, fundamentally, to blame. This is validation of the abuser and abandonment of ourselves.

(3) We believe that the only person in the situation who has the power to change the interaction and thereby relieve our pain is the abuser, not ourselves. We see our only power as limited to trying to get the abuser to stop being abusive. Therefore, we appeal for help to the abuser who, by definition, is unable to respond. This is abandonment of power to the abuser.

The next step is crucial. The struggle outside becomes the struggle inside. *We begin to abuse ourselves exactly as we have been abused.*

The victim/abuser dance is internalized in the self in the form of self-criticism, self-denigration, and self-hate. The essential core of emotional abuse is the inability to stand behind oneself - to feel one's feelings, to defend one's values and perceptions, to speak one's truth. It is the inability to empathize with oneself and be a sympathetic witness to one's own pain. Instead, one mirrors the abuser by attacking oneself in the manner one has been attacked. In fact, we often up the ante. It is well known that we are usually harder on ourselves than others, even our worst abusers, have ever been. The worst form of emotional abuse is self-abuse.

One of the most powerful contributing factors to the mystification of the victim - because it is so devious and yet so undeniably widespread - is the feeling of envy - most particularly, the envy of significant others in the mirroring circle of the family. Its modus operandi is to take what is a positive aspect of a person and twist it into a fault. While the admiration which is contained within the envy gets missed, the hatred and resentment find their mark and become internalized in the person who is the target of another's envious feelings. Over and over I have heard clients criticize what seem to be their best assets and feel crippled in what seem to be their strengths. Beautiful women feel ugly, smart ones stupid, conscientious hard-working men feel lazy, and extremely moral people feel corrupt. One could say that what we are witnessing here is a compensating pendulum swing toward the polar opposite of whatever quality they possess, just as we saw in the case of grandiosity and inferiority or compliance and defiance. Indeed, this may well be true. But when we delve down into the roots of this compensation, we often find green-eyed envy slithering around.

The child may be directly maligned for his or her positive qualities or, more covertly, may simply feel a chill, a conspicuous absence of warmth and positive regard. When we discover through the subtle or not-so-subtle reactions of others that a part of us gets a negative reception, we will conclude that this part is intrinsically defective or bad. Not seeing that the defect lies in the other, we will internalize it as a source of shame. Precisely that about ourselves which could - and should - be most appreciated, we will come to hate. And if our very existence provokes envy in others, we will come to hate that too. In a particularly cruel twist of irony, the admiration of others, unseen through the screen of envy, may end up feeding the most profound experience of self-hatred - the suicidal urge.

If we are unfortunate enough to get under the control of the psychiatric establishment, as I was at age twenty-three following my unsuccessful suicide attempt, we will have the opportunity to reenact our own abuse in a form professionally designed and solicitously presented as "for our own good." It begins with the suspension of our rights as a human being as we descend from being a person to the status of being a psychiatric case.

* * *

The head honcho of the Psych ward was the Chief Psychiatrist, who was also the therapist assigned to me. He was a very busy man. Sometimes a day or two would go by without his seeing me at all.

I wouldn't have minded, since I did not like him very much, except for the rule that I could not go out unless he gave permission and he would not give permission unless he saw me. I had to wait sometimes all day, not knowing whether or not he would grant me an audience.

I'd pace the halls, waiting. I remember thinking to myself that I must have looked the perfect image of a mental patient as I paced the halls. But what else was there to do? The TV was always blaring in the common lounge and the room reeked of smoke. The only other patient anywhere near my age would break out shouting and swearing without provocation. It did not help matters much that his hair stuck straight up and he had a wild and crazy look.

The staff discouraged me from reading (me, a Philosophy student who lived in books) because it was "too solitary" they said. I was never allowed to be alone, anywhere, because I was considered a danger to myself. So, like fly paper, they stuck to me. They followed me everywhere, even to the bathroom. My privacy was erased. They herded me along with the other inmates or trailed behind me as I walked the halls. Sometimes they tried to "involve" me in conversations in which I knew they were scrutinizing my every word.

Just once, in strictest confidence, I shared a poem with a nurse who seemed to be a person I could trust. My poem was brought up in the next session by the Chief Psychiatrist. From then on, I retreated behind a Largactil-like glaze that was the norm on the ward. And I never made that mistake again.

Secretly I concluded that truth was not something they could deal with there. I learned pretty fast that the only way to get along there and, ultimately, to get **out** of there, was to play strictly by the rules. Rule Number One was that the psychiatrist had all the power. He decided if I would be allowed to go off the ward for any reason – for a walk around the block or a visit home or an overnight pass. I could not even step on the elevator without his say. It became, somehow, a matter of urgency for me to get off that ward, to have some visible proof that there was a world outside those walls. For a long time after my release, whenever I rode on an elevator, I had a feeling of grace.

This psychiatrist, like my father, was not an easy person to please. He made disparaging remarks about my appearance so I dressed up for him. He was frequently dissatisfied with my responses so I tried to improve. He even criticized my drawing of a person, a house, and a tree. Presumably, they didn't tell him what he wanted to know.

In exasperation, he decided to administer a Rorschach using Sodium Amytal. In response to my objections, he earnestly assured me that I would be aware at all times during the test and would remember everything. He also promised that afterwards, the *results would be shared with me. None of this was true. How can we expect a person to heal in an environment in which there was no basis for trust? It was just like my family.*

*In retrospect, it seems apparent that institutional experience forced me underground and reinforced compliance of the false self even more powerfully than my family did. It was the medical extension of the authority of the family. Not only did it **not** promote healing of the underlying pain. It actually retarded healing dramatically by mirroring in the supposed treatment the abuse it purported to treat.*

When they finally released me, I went home, feeling miserable inside but with a smile on my face. It was the middle of the Christmas holidays and most students were still away from school, including my roommate and all my college friends. Home was so uncomfortable for me that I decided to drive back to Michigan and stay in my apartment alone. No one in my family questioned this decision or expressed any concern. I did not question it either. I was just so relieved to reclaim the solitude I had lost.

Somewhere tucked away in my psyche, I held a feeling of failure, as if I had blown my only chance, and I never tried suicide again. But I have never forgotten the experience I had just before my consciousness went black. I saw the luminous image of a beach with rolling waves and I had a feeling of absolute bliss. It was a peace deeper than any I have ever known and in it there was no fear.

Many years later, one night after my mate had left, an anger came up in me that must have been lying in wait for the past twenty-seven years. I found myself screaming inside:

"Why didn't you let me die? Why didn't you take me? Why did you make me go back? Why did you send me away?"

It was as though a voice answered: "It wasn't your time to die. You had to go on with life."

"I get to decide about my own life!" I protested vehemently. "It's my decision!"

"No, it's not," the voice said calmly. "It's mine."

"Who are you to tell me..." I was about to shout when I suddenly stopped in mid-thought. Who am I yelling at, I wondered. The question hung in the space around me. If there is no God, who am I fighting with?

For a defiant type, this may be seen as the prototype of a spiritual conversion.

It is vaguely reminiscent of a poem my mother loved to recite:

> *"Last night I saw upon the stair*
> *the little man who wasn't there.*
> *He wasn't there again today.*
> *Oh, how I wish he'd go away!"*

If God had come back to me after so many years without Him, I certainly did not wish Him to go away. I just wished He had arms. "He does," my mate said on the last occasion he spoke to me, "only they're inside."

* * *

We have said that the abuser is unable to respond to or receive feedback from the victim. The reason is that the abuser has also been victimized. We are victims of victims. This means that in his or her own victimization, the abuser also has:

(1) identified with his or her own abuser,

(2) validated or stood behind the point of view of the abuser,

(3) abandoned his or own power to the abuser.

In these ways, the abuser has been, as it were, "trained" to be insensitive and unresponsive - to refuse to occupy the position he or she has just deserted - namely, the victim position. What might be called "non-empathy training" is at the heart of victimization.

* * *

Inspired by Wallace Stephens,[22] I offer these "Thirteen Ways of Looking at a Blackbird" as a meditation on abuse.

ONE.

He must have been very angry. He got up and ran out of the restaurant. I was astonished! I had never seen him act that way before. I called out his name and he looked back at me, his eyes staring, and kept on going. It was the first of many times I was to watch his angrily retreating back.

TWO.

He is angry at me. He makes me get out of the car and walk the rest of the way home.

THREE.

He is angry at me. He yells: "Go have your abandonment crisis by yourself!" He hears his words and has to laugh.

FOUR.

He is angry at me. He hits the washing machine with a resounding crack. He breaks his hand.

FIVE.

He is angry at me. He stands with his hands on his hips and declares hotly: "Face it! In order to have a complete and fulfilling life, you need me!" I am quick to protest that I do not need him in any way.

SIX.

22 Stephens, Wallace: *Collected Poems*, Alfred Knopf, New York, 1954.

He is angry at me. He walks toward me with his chest puffed out and his shoulders squared. He is not a big man. I start backing up and he keeps coming closer until my back is against the wall. I say: "I want to go upstairs now" and he replies "not until we've talked." I try to dodge past him and he blocks my way. "We're going to talk now," he says. It is obvious I have no choice.

SEVEN.

He is angry at me. He grabs my arm and twists it just enough to force me to go with him upstairs to the bedroom. He sets me down on the bed. He closes the bedroom door and locks it. "Now we will talk" he says.

EIGHT.

He is angry at me. I escape to the bedroom and I close the door. The closed door is meant to be a message to him, like one of those hotel room signs hung with a string on the doorknob: "Please Do Not Disturb." I tell myself I am safe here. No armed words to pierce me. No condemning eyes to see my tears. I begin to relax. Suddenly the door is flung open without a knock and he walks in.

NINE.

He is angry at me. I have a lock on the door now. I sit on the bed facing the door, hugging my knees, telling myself "it's okay; he can't come in." He knocks twice sharply and I do not answer. I hold my breath. "Now he will go away," I whisper to myself. He goes away. A moment later he comes back with a screwdriver and pries open the door lock. He walks in. I am frozen. He gets his toothbrush and brushes his teeth very thoroughly. Then he leaves the room.

TEN.

He is angry at me. He dumps out my briefcase, scattering my case notes on the floor. When he sees my horrified expression, he kicks them around with both feet.

ELEVEN.

He is angry at me. He goes outside to his car. I hope he is leaving. I chain-lock the door. He comes back and finds the door locked and rings the doorbell. I do not answer. He rings and rings and rings. Then he steps back and kicks the door with both feet. The chain-lock bursts off the door frame. He walks in.

TWELVE.

He is angry at me. He stalks out of the restaurant and leaves me with the bill to pay. When I arrive home, he is clearing a space in his car for the things he is about to pack. He stomps up to the front door and is about to go in. I am afraid for the children and try to block his way. He throws me down on the cement and I crack my skull.

THIRTEEN.

He is angry at me. He comes near me and I start screaming. He hasn't done anything yet.

* * *

You would be wrong to dismiss this man as simply cruel. This is either/or thinking. Reality is not so neat.

He is also one of the most sensitive, empathic and (yes) loving men you'd ever meet. Nor is he alone in possessing diametrically opposing qualities. As the abuser, so the victim.

One becomes the other on the pendulum of life.

*   *   *

Ask him how I used to rant and rave and stamp my feet. How I could be as unstoppable in the verbal sphere as he was in the physical. Once I got hold of an issue, I would not let it go. I would pursue my point with dogged determination and the force of all that logical artillery I had perfected as a Philosophy major in graduate school until he was reduced to sputtering a two-word profanity in place of an intelligible retort.

What really pushed my buttons was his feigned indifference to me. He had perfected the art of nonchalance, of appearing unaffected and cool.

The highlight of his performance was his remarkable ability to fall asleep. No matter how tense the atmosphere or how charged the scene, he could drop off in minutes. He would, it seemed, virtually shove his serenity in my face. It was infuriating. When my universe felt like it had collapsed in pieces, he'd say "good night" and turn his back to me. I'd mutter to myself: "How dare he go to sleep when I'm lying here awake! After all, he's the one who..." By the time his breathing changed, I'd be really steamed. "How can that weasel sleep soundly while I sit here, bolt upright, staring at the wall!"

I'd counter his go-to-sleep strategy with my deadly wake-him-up frontal attack. A well-placed poke, an energetic shake, and turning on all the lights generally did the trick. Now he'd be angry that I had woken him up but, realizing that I could keep at him all night, he'd usually shrug himself upright and engage. We'd be two battle-weary soldiers scraping ourselves out of bed early the next morning.

From first-hand experience, I would conclude that sleep deprivation plays a much larger and more serious role in chronic conflictual relationships than has generally been realized to date. If it can be used to brainwash and induce psychosis, it is equally potent as a mind-bending, mood-altering and confidence-eroding component of marital strife. My son's caricature of adult life seems to sum it up: "You go to bed late, you get up early and you're cranky all day."

Perhaps the single most pressing impetus for couple's therapy is the hope of getting a good night's sleep!

* * *

Let me summarize my position. The point that needs to be made first and loudly is that much of what passes as normal interaction is abusive. We need to start with the naming of the crime. What makes emotional abuse so difficult to identify is that we minimize it, normalize it, and blame the victim.

Because we are fused with the other, we do not see our boundary violations *as* violations. We think we have the right to act as we do. Because we confuse what is *normal* with what is *acceptable*, we learn to distance from and invalidate our pain. Charlie Brown was right when he said "Pain hurts!" And abuse *is* abusive. The pain is real and it is *not* the victim's fault.

But the victim does play a part. Beyond any awareness or intention, our characteristic victim ways of responding broadcast helplessness and passivity. We project an unconscious expectation of abuse. We are so identified with the other that appropriate ways of protecting ourselves do not occur to us as options. We walk straight into the lion's mouth. To risk the anger or disapproval of the other is too threatening to our tenuous sense of self. Therefore, we remain vulnerable. Unfortunately, in accord with Murphy's law of psychology that whatever we run away from we will run into, as victims, we bring out the very anger and contempt we are trying to escape.

Not only does victim behavior provoke anger on the conscious level, but it also triggers in the abuser an unconscious memory of the helplessness felt when they were victims and a defensive reaction against this memory. Thus what I hate in you is the helplessness I have experienced in myself. My abusiveness is a rejection of that helplessness in both you and me.

To understand the anger of the abuser is not in any way to condone the abuse. It cannot be condoned. But we can condemn the action and at the same time strive to see the person behind the action, the fear behind the rage.

It has been recognized in the literature that victim and abuser are reciprocal roles in a deadly dance, but what has often not been acknowledged is that these roles alternate. Victim becomes abuser and the abuser victimized. We prefer to keep things separate and dichotomized like the white hats and the black hats in a cowboy movie that proclaim unequivocally who is the good guy and who the bad. But reality does not divide up that way. Each person has their viewpoint and their own slice of truth. Though a particular action may be blameworthy, no one person will be all bad or wholly to blame. Inside of each of us is the capacity to hurt, to do harm, and to hate. It is when we deny this capacity in ourselves that we are the most dangerous and when abuse cloaks itself in the guise of acceptability that we have the most to fear.

Part Three

Silencing the Superego

To my superego demons:

This book is me . . .
                        no matter what you think.

The picture before us is an undeniably gloomy one, reminiscent of wry comments like "Life's a bitch and then we die." The charade that poses as "love" becomes the fusion of two false selves who each manipulate to get the other to be what we think we need them to be. In this woeful exchange, each of us ends up hungry and alienated, not only from the other but, perhaps more tragically, from ourselves.

The paradox is that the person who is thus "loved" is not me (the false self) while the me (shadow) is not loved. We are reminded of Groucho Marx's telling remark: "I would not want to belong to a club that would have *me* for a member!" No wonder, then, that we become angry, hurt, lonely and afraid, fractured selves longing to be whole.

What is the way out then? What are we to do? In this section, we will begin to address the process of healing and the steps that need to be taken if therapy is to act as a bridge to reintegration of the self.

As stated earlier, methodologies may vary but the steps will be the same and will be present in some form in all therapy which is effective in bringing about change. For the purpose of conceptualization, we will address these steps as if they were discrete and sequential, much as language is. However, the lived process is not this way. As anyone who has been in therapy will attest, we move forward and fall backward repeatedly. The steps interpenetrate. It is more like a spiraling than a linear progression. We realize and forget again, many times over, before the awareness gels. And sometimes the distance from awareness to action can seem an interminable one. But however long and circuitous, however many twists and turns it takes, there is a discernible path to be followed and it is this path we will proceed to trace.

Once we understand what causes splitting and damage to the self, we can see that reintegration and healing will be the exact reverse of this process.

The opposite of fusion is bonding. I define bonding as

"acceptance of the other as they are." By implication, inner bonding is acceptance of the self as it is. Since, at bottom, it is the rejection of self and other that causes splitting, the healing of this discord will be through acceptance of the self and other as they are.

This becomes our principle eleven:

11. Bonding is acceptance of the other as they are; inner bonding is acceptance of the self as it is. Healing is through bonding.

I believe that the essential ingredient in effective psychotherapy is the provision of an opportunity for bonding. It is the environment of acceptance by the therapist that enables the client to learn to accept him or herself.

This means that Carl Rogers[23] was right when he identified unconditional positive regard as the *sine qua non* of therapeutic change *so long as* unconditional regard is understood to include acknowledgment and acceptance of the shadow self which has been disowned by the client. Otherwise, support operates at the level of the false self and does not effect any deep transformation. It is in developing empathy with the repressed feelings of the child that the therapist builds a bridge to reintegration, and it is precisely that identification which was formerly abandoned as too threatening that needs to be facilitated in therapy. Within the context of a holding environment, the "uncrossing" of the cross-over becomes possible and, through that shift in perspective, the recovery of our abandoned selves.

The Bonding Cycle is summarized in Diagram B. Fusion is contrasted with bonding in Diagram C.

I see the development of a sympathetic witness as the core of therapeutic bonding. As the name suggests, "sympathetic

23 See Rogers, Carl: *On Becoming a Person*, Houghton Mifflin, Boston, 1961; *Freedom to Learn*, Charles E. Merrill, Columbus, Ohio, 1969, "Client-Centered Psychotherapy" in *Comprehensive Textbook of Psychiatry, Vol. 11*, Williams & Wilkins, Baltimore, 1975.

witness" is a bringing together of two elements: sympathizing and witnessing. The witnessing component is essentially (but not restrictively) cognitive, while the sympathizing is essentially (but not restrictively) affective. We can see it as a combination of empathy and compassion.

Empathy is defined as "the intellectual identification with or vicarious experiencing of the feelings, thoughts or attitudes of another person" — in this case, of the client in their childhood past. It involves the reconstruction of the truth of the child's experience in their family of origin, however unpalatable that truth. Through a process of demythologizing and demystifying, we come to face the illusions that we retained from the cross-over to the parent perspective. In this process, the idealization of the parent breaks down and we begin to see the discrepancy in ourselves between false self and true feelings. In surfacing the repressed feelings of the child, we learn to accept the shadow parts of both self and other that were previously disowned.

Diagram B

BONDING CYCLE	
THERAPIST	CLIENT
Bonds with the client	Bonds with the therapist
Develops empathy with client	Develops empathy with him or
Becomes a sympathetic witness	herself
for the client	Becomes a sympathetic witness
Accepts the shadow of the	to self
client	Breaks fusion with parents
	Becomes empathic to others
	Accepts his or her own shadow
HEALING CYCLE	

Diagram C
COMPARISON OF FUSION AND BONDING

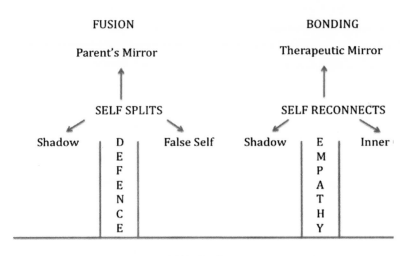

* * *

The Wizard of Oz has always held a terrible fascination for me ever since, at age six, my parents left me alone to watch it in a movie theater. After all (they must have reasoned), it was a children's movie so what was there to fear? They obviously did not foresee flying monkeys, thundering wizards, and cackling witches.

That movie haunted me for years. Even in my training as a therapist, I remember Jorge Rosner, my Gestalt trainer, shouting at me: "The Gestalt Institute is NOT the wicked witch of the West!"

But the effect did not wear off. Once, with shock, I saw the same actress who had played the witch in a mild-mannered role in a commercial on TV. I never voiced my secret conviction that it was the wicked witch of the west traveling incognito promoting Maxwell House coffee!

I always identified with Dorothy, the little girl who was trying to go home. I had yet to fully embrace the knowledge that there is no way to go back home. No way, that is, to meet those needs that *were not met in childhood, no way to find in mere human beings the idealized parents we seek.*

My unconscious tried to nudge me along by providing me with a dream. In it, the witch was standing behind a screen with her profile in silhouette, just as I had seen her as a child. A voice in the dream announced summarily, as if it were delivering an editorial comment to a moron:

"The wicked witch of the west is ... **your mother!**"

I thought I had finished with the witch then.

* * *

In general usage, compassion is understood to be "a feeling of deep sympathy and sorrow for another's suffering or misfortune accompanied by a desire to alleviate the pain or remove its cause." Certainly, caring about the suffering of the child is a priority in therapeutic bonding. But the false self is often contracted against experiencing this pain. The implication for therapy is that rather than reinforcing our defensive contraction, it will be necessary for us to surface and re-experience that pain. Thus, therapy may seem, in its initial stages, to increase rather than decrease our pain. On this point, A.H. Almaas writes:

> Usually compassion is seen as a desire to alleviate someone else's pain. Compassion is experienced as a desire to help. We feel compassionate when we see someone hurt... So we connect compassion with pain and hurt. However, this is only the elementary level of compassion. The real function of compassion is not to eliminate suffering, but to lead a person to the truth. Much of the time, the truth is painful or scary. Compassion makes it possible to tolerate the hurt and fear... The compassion doesn't eliminate the pain; it makes the pain meaningful, makes it part of the truth, makes it tolerable.
>
> This way of viewing compassion makes a tremendous difference in our lives. Seeing compassion as a guide to the

truth rather than something to alleviate hurt, can change
the way we behave toward ourselves, our friends, everyone.
Although it may seem a subtle difference, the one perspective
will take you away from truth and the other will take you
towards it. One will keep you unconscious, one will help you
learn the truth.[24]

It is rather like a poster I recall of a rag doll going through
the ringer of an old-fashioned washing machine. The caption
read: "The truth shall make you free. But first it shall make
you miserable."

*   *   *

I see the Wizard of Oz as a myth of individuation. Each of
the characters comes to the Great Other, the Wizard, hoping to
be supplied with what they are missing. The Wizard is, literally, a
projection on a screen. In the course of fulfilling their mission, each
character discovers the qualities in themselves that they thought they
lacked. The message is that what we seek in the other is to be found
in ourselves.

It is only at the point that they have become what they hoped to
be that the projection breaks down. The curtain is pulled back and
they discover the little old man behind the screen. It is a moment
of deep disillusionment when the Wizard turns out to be merely
human. He has no power to bestow on them the state of being
they seek but he can help them acknowledge who they already are.
Perhaps psychotherapists are a lot like wizards in this respect.

*   *   *

As the therapist models compassion for the suffering of the
disowned child and encourages recognition of the underlying
source, we learn to feel compassion for ourselves, particularly
for those aspects of self that were previously rejected. This
new mirroring offered by the therapeutic relationship allows
us to be more fully ourselves, without the need for disguise or

24 Almaas, A.H.: *Diamond Heart Book One: Elements of the Real in Man*, Diamond
Books, Almaas Publications, Berkeley, 1987, pages 91-93.

deception. As we learn to honor our own feelings, thoughts, perceptions and values, the split begins to heal. We are growing a new sympathetic witness inside ourselves that replaces the judgmental parent we hosted up till now.

Because we are no longer fused with the parent, we will no longer need to be, or not be, what was expected of us. We are free to be ourselves. The desire to care for ourselves leads us to learn better ways to protect and advocate for the self. In therapy, this learning is characterized as the development of healthy boundaries.[25] As self-acceptance and self-protection grow, we become less defensive and more able to extend our empathy and compassion outward to others. Fusion thus yields to trust and trust opens the heart to love.

Principle twelve states:

12. Therapeutic bonding is becoming a sympathetic witness. It is a manifestation of love.

The love I speak of now is not the fused "love" of manipulation and control but the experience of communion. It presupposes two selves who are separate and have achieved some measure of wholeness and self-love. They are drawn together not out of need but out of what my mentor, Andrew Feldmar, calls "a delight in the other as they are." [26] This is the love of non-attachment, non-possession, and non-demand. It takes us from the domain of power and control to the heart level, from morality to spirituality. Through my compassion for myself as a human being, I feel my connection with all human beings and with the drama that is played out for each of us in our journey to self.

The logic of the therapeutic journey is encapsulated in these twelve principles. To summarize:

25 On developing boundaries see, for example, Katharine, Anne: *Boundaries: Where You End and I Begin*, Parkside Publishing Company, Park Ridge, Illinois, 1991.
26 Comment by Andrew Feldmar in a lecture entitled "Children and Morality", Vancouver, March 1993.

PRINCIPLES OF THE THERAPEUTIC JOURNEY:

1. The self is formed in relationship.

2. Boundaries are the interface of self and other in relationship.

3. Self-image is the result of mirroring by the other.

4. Each person needs to be loved and to matter.

5. Each child wants to believe that his or her parents are okay.

6. The child identifies with the parent and loses empathy with him or herself.

7. The false self is the child's accommodation to his or her parents' image. The shadow is the disowned, unacceptable part of the self.

8. Self-hate is the rejection of the self as it is. It includes both poles of narcissism: grandiosity and inferiority.

9. Fusion is the failure to perceive the other as a separate self. It is, therefore, a boundary violation.

10. Fusion leads to abuse of the other; self-hate leads to abuse of the self.

11. Bonding is acceptance of the other as they are; inner bonding is acceptance of the self as it is. Healing is through bonding.

12. Therapeutic bonding is becoming a sympathetic witness. It is a manifestation of love.

*   *   *

Now that we have the general sweep of the therapeutic process, we need to get into the nitty-gritty of moving through each step. We shall begin with the first roadblock in the way of self-acceptance: the Superego.

The Superego is the exponent of values, moralistic standards, expectations and demands. It tells you what you *should* be, drives you to keep on trying, and berates you when you fall short. It is the mainstay of the defensive structure that supports the false self. It is the voice in my head that would say, echoing my father when I got ninety-seven out of a hundred on a school test: "What happened to the other three marks?" Is it any wonder I became a perfectionist?

The Superego is the repository of all those negative judgments that have affected our self-image, particularly those that have come from primary caregivers and significant others in the family. Therefore, it will be a window into the way we have been emotionally abused. What we have internalized of the judgments of others, often in the precise words or tone of voice we heard them, will be replicated in the Superego. It is the abuser who has taken up residence inside of us.

It is staggering when it finally dawns on us that the bulk of emotional abuse is created, developed and sustained by *ourselves*. Someone makes a remark we interpret as critical in the morning and we chew on it, turn it over in our minds, and suck on its bitterness all day. We let it burn in our brains all evening and keep it recycling through our wakefulness all night.

Who torments us this way? It is our own Superego reviling us mercilessly. Or suppose we were told thirty years ago that we were unattractive or dumb. It is our own constant repetition of this condemnation that pounds this judgment into us, thirty years of repetition that produces the debilitating depression we have experienced each day. To our dismay, we have to admit: we are doing it to ourselves. To our horror, we have to recognize: the enemy is within.

* * *

When, in the wake of my mate's desertion, reality rolled over me, my self split.

*On the outside, I got up and starting coping – furiously. I was catapulted into survival mode and I work assiduously until the wee hours of the morning, day after day. Unpacking, setting up a new household, dealing with a new house, new equipment, a new neighborhood, looking after my children, working with lawyers, running my practice, taking in foreign students, feeding them and my family, struggling frantically to reduce the debt load he had left me with. I was busy **all** the time.*

On the inside, visible to no one, I lay there paralyzed and bled. My inner world was black, my grief unbearable. The only relief was in fantasy. There my mate became like a permanent lodger in my mind who walked around in bedroom slippers and made himself a cup of tea. I obsessed about him night and day. I talked with him, walked with him, slept with him, cried with him. I, who had never trusted in his presence, found in his absence a reliable source of nurturance.

*It was a dubious triumph that I finally achieved object constancy only after the object of my affection had withdrawn. The most tragic irony was that I only really **knew** I had been loved when I was loved no more. So deep was my distrust, so barren my beginnings, that I never took in the reality of his love until he had taken it away.*

*And he took it away absolutely. He would not even **talk** to me. He moved on his life, taking up with a woman he had loved before, but the fat lady never sang for me. I was in love and I didn't know how to get out. My heart stayed in the open position. Pleasure became a memory. Music a pain. Sex an impossibility. Out of desperation (and quitting my better judgment), I went to see a psychiatrist.*

With that raised-eyebrow look that psychiatrists perfect, he challenged me: " So you plan to die of unrequited love?" he inquired condescendingly.

"I may die of unrequited love," I thought, "but I won't die in therapy with you." And I quit.

But years dragged on. My secret longing never waned. One day my Superego launched a full-scale attack.

"You stupid twit! Look what you did! You blew it! The most blissful love that God could offer and you destroyed it! You threw it away! You spoiled it! How could you be so stupid!"

On and on it went, upbraiding me. It had no forgiveness, no mercy, no empathy. Suddenly it struck me that all the years of pain and misery were a punishment meted out **by me**. *Even at the worst of his hatred and the depth of his rage, my mate could not have devised for me a torture more horrendous than the one I had been giving myself.*

* * *

You can think of the Superego as a part inside that is *not* your friend. It is a long-time resident in your psyche who is always busy ordering you around.

To give credit where credit is due, it needs to be acknowledged that its guidance has been instrumental in ensuring your survival up to this point. But, ultimately, it will be necessary to wage war on or, at least, to dethrone this part of the personality if we are to transcend the old stuck place and move beyond survival to growth. It is only by learning to silence the Superego that we can open the door to the shadow and to its integration into the self.

Becoming aware of the persistent nagging presence of the Superego is a decidedly unpleasant but necessary task. We will notice immediately how remarkably adept we are at remaining oblivious to the constant negative chatter going on in our heads. It will require a special effort to tune in and turn the volume up.

One of my clients used a traffic counter to keep track of the ongoing barrage of criticisms she experienced in an average day. Another allotted herself a maximum of five minutes per day to voice into the mirror any complaints she had about herself and then she would write them down afterward in her journal. Others recorded all the negative statements they heard in their heads in a fifteen minute period three times a day for a week. You may well be astounded, as they were, at the sheer magnitude of instances of self-rebuke.

An unfailingly powerful exercise I have used in workshops is to invite participants to mill around making non-verbal contact while playing a stream of self-doubting and self-deprecating tapes in their heads. Then I ask them to contrast this experience with the contact they make while playing self-nurturing and self-affirming tapes in their heads. Without exception, people have reported a radical shift directly reflective of their negative or positive self-statements in their perceptions of others as well as of themselves. The principle of the self-fulfilling prophecy holds sway here. How we see others is, for better and for worse, largely a reflection of how we see ourselves.

The Superego is more than just an inner and private tormentor affecting our self-perceptions. It is also a potent shaper of the reality we encounter outside ourselves. No wonder, then, that the times we most desperately need the world to respond to us with support and beneficence, it seems to mock and jab at us in the heinous face of our worst fears. The only way to regain mastery of both our external world and our inner selves is to challenge the entrenched power of the Superego.

A simple (but not easy) method of working with the Superego is to follow these three steps which I call the **ABC**"s. This method has been distilled from a Diamond Heart workshop, presented by Michael Torreson, and liberally interpreted by me.

Step **A** is to identify the primary Superego messages for each one of us individually. Fortunately, there are only a few, maybe four or five for each person, and all the rest are merely variations on each theme. To discover these primary messages, it is necessary to listen closely to the background prattle that is going on all the time, much like elevator music but not so pleasant to the ears. We can then extrapolate from the multiplicity of daily criticisms and harangues the major points of vulnerability that form the basis of attack. Or, alternatively, we can target specific situations that produced defensive reactions in us and draw out these same points of vulnerability contextually.

Each negative message will be encoded in very idiosyncratic language derived from our individual histories. Thus, the exact wording will be very much our own and unique. Some messages are directed more at our physical appearance, others at our character, our accomplishments, or at our overall value. At times we may actually hear our parent's words, their turn of phrase, or tone of voice. For instance, it is not surprising that one of my persistent Superego messages is: "Nobody wants you. You're a pain in the butt!" It is unnerving to acknowledge how much we are haunted by unfriendly ghosts from the past.

Some examples that may call up your own ghosts are offered below.

1. For god's sakes, don't be like your mother!
[i.e. depressed, a wimp, a nag, or ...]

2. There you go! You blew it! That's just like you to screw up again!

3. Don't let people see you're hurt [scared, angry]. They won't like you anymore.

4. You're so selfish! [lazy, stupid, weak...]

5. Grow up! Get on with it! Who cares how you feel?

6. You are such a loser! No one loves you and no one ever will.

7. See! I knew it all along! You're just being used and exploited again.

8. You deserve what you get. You've never been any good. You'll never amount to anything.

9. You're hopeless. No matter how you try, you'll never get out of here.

10. People will find out sooner or later what a terrible person you really are.

These messages and others like them represent the first wave of Superego attack. Depending on the history, they will be more or less nasty, brutal or contemptuous. But however harsh and rejecting, at least this attack is frontal. We can see where it is coming from and who is packing the guns.

There is another form of attack that is more insidious. Rather than a screeching harpy, it whispers seductively in your ear. It is reasonable, subtle and calm. When you find yourself knocked down and flattened, you don't even know where the attack came from. The bait it uses to lure you to its counsel is your own ego ideal. Do you want to be rich, well known, successful? Or kind, generous, and good? A good mother? A devoted husband? A thoughtful daughter? Or a trustworthy friend? Is your goal to be integrated, whole, and healthy? Or is spiritual enlightenment your end? Whatever inspires you as a model becomes the Superego's ploy to shape you in its image and make you feel guilty for who you are.

*　*　*

Every Friday night my mother cooked a chicken. In my growing up, chickens came whole. You couldn't buy packages of just wings or drumsticks as you can today. Each chicken has, as its natural endowment, only two wings, which are quite small and have a good deal of bone. Just the same, wings were my favorite part.

Every Friday night my mother let me have the wings on the

chicken. She knew they were the part I liked the best. Luckily, nobody else in the family seemed to want them anyway. So I felt particularly blessed.

Even with the exceptions, like the nights when we were somewhere else or they were away in Florida or the two summer months when I was at camp, you can imagine how many Friday nights there were in twenty- some years of my life from early childhood until the age of twenty-three. That was the time when my mother and I sat in the kitchen having a conversation that meandered around to the subject of favorite foods.

I reiterated my well-known preference for chicken wings and hers, long established and unquestioned, for the breast.

"Actually, the breast was never my favorite," she confided, to my stunned surprise. "In fact, I never really liked it all that much. I always loved the wings but I let you have them because I knew they were your favorite."

It was as if, at that moment, all the wings I had ever eaten marched before my eyes, solemnly saluting like grim soldiers, paying homage to her silent sacrifice. She was noble. I was base, mortified, a creature of sin, a mere mortal full of guilt and chicken wings.

* * *

It is important to recognize that the therapy process can become an unwitting broker for the Superego, as can any spiritual training program. In fact, this is the place where healing all too often gets derailed. Instead of a holding environment in which the process of unfolding is honored, whatever form it takes, we may set up a new set of pressures for the client to unfold *this* way, to become who they are but do it quickly or in accord with this model of integration or that.

For example, in my Gestalt therapy training, we were admonished to be who we were, but twice a year we were evaluated on the progress we were making. Continuance in the program was contingent on this evaluation and how we were seen to have progressed. Nor was this an idle threat.

Twenty-four students embarked on the program and three years later, only eleven managed to "be themselves" adequately to graduate.

Admittedly, this was a program dedicated to the training of therapists, not a program of therapy itself. But how often do we inadvertently carry this same double message into our therapy and convey to our clients, directly or indirectly, that there is a *right* way to be or a *right* way to grow and that we know this way?

In the case of the Psych ward, figuring out the psychiatrist's way became my path to freedom and I knew without question that if I didn't follow his way, I would not get out. Is it so far afield to imagine that we may convince ourselves that if our clients do not follow our admonitions, they will not heal?

Of course, not all therapy is done on a locked ward and thus, one may retort, our clients are free to go. However, this supposed freedom is, more often than not, reactive. Depending on their style, compliant clients will likely accommodate to our pressure and thereby prolong their treatment, while defiant clients will likely bolt and terminate prematurely. Have we done either one a favor? Once I told a cancer client whom I dearly loved that if she didn't get angry, she would be at risk of getting her cancer back. She got angry at me and left. Does this mean I was "right"?

The ego ideal is very seductive. Have you ever spent time in a spiritual community in which everybody is trying so hard to be loving, cheerful and nice? As well as deeply compromising the soul's need for truth, it hurts the smile muscles at the sides of your mouth.

Ram Dass[27] tells a story that is instructive here about the moment he came to the realization that his guru could read his mind. With that realization, all the most repulsive, disgusting, and humiliating thoughts he had ever had began to stream through his head as he sat there, just a few meters from his guru's feet. Overwhelmed by shame, Ram Dass looked up

27 Ram Dass: *On Relationships*, (audiotape) Windstar Series, The Soundworks, Arlington, Virginia, 1984.

at that moment to find Maharishi looking down at him with a gaze of all-encompassing love. Would that we could look into the mirror of our own selves without pretense, without hiding, and be lovingly received in that way.

For most of us, this sort of unconditional love is well beyond our reach.

Compliant people want, above all, to be liked and approved of. Their ideal is Miss Nice Lady or Mr. Nice Guy. They try to convince themselves that they really are as accommodating and agreeable as they pretend to be. Therefore, they go along, sometimes for weeks, months or years, being ingratiating and pleasing others without any conscious recognition that there is a problem here. Their resentment grows and festers beneath the surface until it reaches a boiling point. Then one day they just explode or walk out, never to return. This is the meaning of the old adage: "Beware the doormat rises!"

Defiant people strive to maintain the illusion of independence. Their superegos terrorize them with visions of weakness, helplessness, and neediness. "Don't be a wimp" is a message that could be carved above their front doors. It is often as much a shock to them as it is to their significant others to see the collapse of such apparently self-sufficient beings when their dependency needs are triggered and cannot be met.

To avoid dealing with the resentment buried in compliance or the neediness masked in defiance, we prefer to tolerate the daily recriminations of the Superego whose function it is to keep our defenses in place. The less aware we are of this tyranny, the more effective it will be.

Hence, **Step B** is designed to heighten our awareness of the characteristic bodily symptoms that occur when we have been under siege by the Superego, either directly or indirectly, so that we are more likely to take notice. What we can register we can rectify or, at least, resist.

To discover what symptoms you experience when your Superego assaults you, try this experiment. Get a person you trust to stand behind you and feed you the messages you have identified in Step A, coaching them on the intonation and volume that sound right to you. Then simply notice how your body responds. You may recognize some of the symptoms identified by others in the sample list below:

* feeling paralyzed and like a zombie
* feeling blank and dazed
* becoming tired and sleepy
* feeling teary and wanting to cry
* my throat lumps up and my voice is choked
* my face gets red
* my heart speeds up
* I can't think straight
* I am unable to make a decision
* I stare out the window pathetically
* I run to the refrigerator
* I start craving junk food
* my hands shake
* I stutter when I speak
* I feel shaky inside
* my shoulders get tense and I hunch over
* I get antsy and restless
* my stomach knots
* I feel like screaming
* I clench my teeth
* my jaw tightens
* my voice sounds little and weak
* I feel nauseous
* I feel dizzy
* I want to run away and hide.

We can almost glimpse behind these descriptions the terrorized child recoiling from the attacks of the critical parent within. By becoming cognizant of our bodily responses, we can prepare to fight back.

In **Step C**, we begin to experiment with strategies of counter-attack. We develop a set of statements that will refute, silence, or overpower the Superego. We then proceed to test their effectiveness in response to the Step A messages we hear. We will know we are successful when the voice is stilled, however temporarily, and the symptoms abate.

The responses that work to silence the Superego may not be the most articulate, sophisticated or smart. For example, I found that sticking out my tongue and covering my ears often worked. The litmus test is when you reconnect with your power and the Superego stops its attack. Therefore, it is important that you practice various approaches until you find the one that works for you.

Some responses that many have found effective are detailed below. I offer a generic description of each response and then some sample vocalizations to give you an idea of how they would sound.

1. EXPLETIVES

In ordinary life, when we want someone to shut up or go away, we may use expletives with or without cursing, sometimes accompanied by gestures, to drive our point home. Some examples are:

"Get lost! Take a hike! Shut up! Be quiet! Leave me alone! "

and others that may appear in your minds but not in the book.

2. UNDERMINING THE AUTHORITY OF THE SUPEREGO

We are listening to a voice inside that tells us what to do but have we ever really questioned who this voice is and what right it has to dictate to us? We can ask:

"Who cares what you think? You don't know what you're

talking about! Who are you to judge? I don't have to listen to you!

3. REOWNING OUR RIGHT TO HAVE OUR FEELINGS

We know that the Superego originates in the family. Many families have injunctions against certain feelings or against having feelings at all. Therefore we can respond:
" It's okay to be hurt [angry, scared, sad or ...]. Let me have my feelings!

4. IDENTIFYING THE MANIPULATIVE PLOY OF THE SUPEREGO

The Superego will often be modeled on a parent who used manipulative strategies or games to get the behavior that was desired. This same style of manipulation will be present in your Superego messages today.
We can fight back with:
"Don't try to make me feel guilty! [ashamed, bad, inadequate, helpless or ...]

5. IDENTIFYING THE SOURCE OF THE SUPEREGO MESSAGES

Recognizing the manipulative strategies of the Superego will often pinpoint the original source of the attack.
We may say:
"Hello, mother, so you're still trying to make me feel guilty!" or "Hello, Dad, so you're still trying to put me down!

6. DENYING THE TRUTH OF THE SUPEREGO MESSAGES

The Superego can be looked at as "the used car salesman

of the mind", meaning that what it says is not to be counted upon. In most cases, what it says is simply false. Even if there were a germ of truth, it has been so blown out of proportion that the generalization it draws has no support in truth.

We may choose to make a frontal attack by asserting:
"That's not true! I'm NOT selfish [lazy, stupid or ...]

7. AFFIRMATION OF SELF

We may simply bypass the content of the Superego messages and reassert our support of ourselves. In this way, we replace the critical voice in our heads with that of the sympathetic witness.

We repeat:
" I like me. I'm a good person. I'm fine the way I am."

8. SOOTHING MANTRA & COMFORT GESTURE

Sometimes the best tactic may be to drown out the Superego with a positive repeating phrase combined with a comfort gesture. Often these gestures come from childhood like the afore-mentioned sucking my thumb. They may include: patting your chest, hugging yourself, going into foetal position, rocking, stroking your thighs or arms, all the while chanting a mantra over and over to yourself.

My favorite is:
I love you (to self), I love you, I love you, I love you.

9. HUMOR

Humor offers a unique perspective. In order to find something funny, we need to be detached. We need to step back from the situation in order to laugh at it. This detachment implies that we are no longer buying into the Superego point of view but are able to rise above it. When it is possible to have a sense of humor about a Superego message, we have transcended it. At the same time, we get to enjoy the benefits of a lightened mood.

10. COMBINATION APPROACH

Do not feel restricted to one method at a time. You can come out with guns blazing using a combination approach.

When practicing Step C with a client one day, she bowled over my Superego objections with an artillery fire that sounded like this:

"Shut up! You don't know what you're talking about. I'm fine the way I am and I'm not listening to you. You sound like my mother and she was always wrong about me. That's all b.s.! Get lost! I love me, I love me, I love me."

I wish I could report that using this methodology stops the Superego for good. Unfortunately, this does not seem to be the case. The frequency of the attacks will diminish. The harshness will subside. If we do get caught in a Superego trap, we will have the memory of having defeated it before and thus will have an easier time freeing ourselves.

However, the Superego seems to be a faithful, though unwanted, companion in our lives. It may go dormant but can rise up to pounce at any time. Therefore, it is essential to remain watchful and aware of what is going on in your mind. Think of these steps as a survival kit that you will be a constant practice in your life.

When cultivated as a discipline, these three steps are remarkably effective in counteracting the critical dictates of the Superego and its Gestapo-like regime.

* * *

We could address the same issue in a more provocative, roguish or impudent way. Sometimes I think we need a little good-hearted irreverence, some spicy boldness, or a streak of racy daring to free us up from all the rigid rules and regulations that have us locked in their stranglehold. We need a way of shaking up the Superego.

My method is simple. Just ask the "Why?" question, or the even less respectable "Why not?" question, when nobody else seems to be doing so. It's sure to add a few corkscrew turns into an otherwise straight-laced road.

"Why?" questions are like moles. Normally, when humans meet a wall, we try to go around it, we check if we can climb over it, we look on either side of it, and then we give up and walk away. Some of us may stay and bang our heads on it. But the mole who meets a wall is undeflected. He simply burrows under it and comes up on the other side. "Why?" questions can take you under walls - prohibitions, objections, remonstrations - in much the same way.

I once had a client who wanted to leave a boring job in the tax department but his Superego was opposed. He had this conversation with the mole:

I have to work in the tax department.
Mole: Why?

I have to pay my rent. . . . .
Mole: Why?

If I didn't pay my rent, I'd have to move and
    I don't want to have to move. . . . .
Mole: Why?

I don't think I could find a cheaper place to
    live in this part of the city and I want to
    live in this part of the city. . . . .
Mole: Why?

I need to be close to my job in the tax department.

Asking "Why?" questions can be explosive. This might be why my sister called me "weird". I can see that this Socratic mole made a startling difference in my life. Some of the questions I asked were:

Why do I have to be nice to people I don't like?

Why can't girls be smart?

Why can't girls be philosophers?

Why do I have to live with my family?

Why do I have to live in the city?

Why do I have to live?

Why can't I give up a tenure-track position?

Why do I have to marry within my religion?

Why do I have to be married to own a house?

Why do I have to be married to have a baby?

Why do I have to be married?

Why do people fight?

Why can't Jewish people have Christmas trees?

Why can't therapists tell their own stories?

Why *not* write a book?

Be careful what questions you ask or you may end up "weird" like me.

* * *

What will happen when the gates are left unguarded and we are no longer constricted and constrained? Will we be like the laboratory rats raised in cages who, when the doors of their cages were opened, sniffed around near the opening and then scuttled back inside? Can we who have been compliant make connection with the rage inside us? Can we who have hidden in defiance embrace the neediness within? We stand at the gates of the shadow, in fear and trembling.

It appears that the more severely we have been abused, the more difficult it will be to face the shadow in ourselves. As therapists, we know that the most defended, skittish, and reactive of clients come out of the most deeply troubled origins. Basic trust is absent and trust forms the bridge to self-acceptance. Therefore, for growth to occur, it becomes imperative for us to create the conditions most conducive to the development of basic trust.

In the therapeutic relationship, we have an optimal environment in which to nurture the growth of basic trust. The therapeutic alliance is, potentially, the most powerful vehicle for making the necessary bridge to basic trust *provided that* the therapist does not unwittingly become aligned with the Superego. Should that occur, therapy will serve to reinforce the false self and become itself an enabler of victimization and self-abuse.

It is this unfortunate result that Alice Miller[28] decried in her critique of psychoanalysis by showing it to be an apology for the parent perspective rather than an advocacy of the child. (And isn't this what happened to me on the Psych ward at age twenty-three?)

For healing to occur, we must learn to align with the child, to become, that is, a sympathetic witness to the child within. The therapist models the witness position for us as clients until we can sustain this perspective on our own. No amount of theorizing or intellectualizing can replace the immediate personal experience of reclaiming the child.

* * *

I worked all day Wednesday until late Wednesday night. It didn't seem remarkable because I got home by nine or ten p.m. while my mate didn't roll in from his work until close to midnight. Compared to him, I seemed fortunate. We both got up early the next morning and worked a normal day.

28 Miller, Alice: *Banished Knowledge: Facing Childhood Injuries*, Doubleday, New York, 1990.

It would be about 5:30 every Thursday afternoon when I would force my weary legs up the endless climb to my home with thoughts of all the chores that lay between me and rest racing through my head. The dinner that had to be cooked and served, the dishes to be cleaned, the dog to be fed and put out, next day's lunches to be made. Stairs up, stairs down, and stairs up again. Children to be bathed and put to bed. Bills to be paid. Plans to arrange. All these, like reaching hands, grabbed at me. I felt pressure in every nerve. My body ached, my head spun, and a voice in me longed to scream "No! I can't do it! It's too much! No, I'm sorry. NO!"

And every Thursday I'd announce to my mate in terms that were unmistakable: "I'm dead tired and I need your help tonight" to a face behind a newspaper. Since I had correctly followed the rules of communication prescribed by my therapy training, I was baffled and confused, never understanding why the upshot was always the same – disappointment and resentment. The "Thursday evening argument" would play out once again.

How long had I been teaching others about the inner child before I actually heard her? The girl on the stairs whining, "It's too much for me. I'm only little." The child on the stairs wailing, "Don't make me do any more! I'm too tired." The victim beseeching, " Help me. Help me.

*I wanted **him** to hear me. I wanted him to care. But I was asking to receive from outside what had to come from within: the acknowledgment, empathy, validation and caretaking.*

Of course, he always let me down. That was the prescribed script. Either he did nothing, or he did it wrong, or he didn't do enough. In retrospect, this was probably inevitable for no one can ever parent us in the ideal way we need or make up to the child for the parenting we missed. I was seeing him as responsible for what I had to do myself – to be responsible (ie. able to respond) to my child within. Without this ability to respond, we remain stuck in the victim role. We cycle around the Karpman triangle[29] searching for a rescuer and finding a persecutor instead.

---

29 Karpman, Stephen B: "Fairy Tales and Script Drama Analysis", *Transactional Analysis Bulletin, VII, No. 26* (April 1968) pages 39-43.

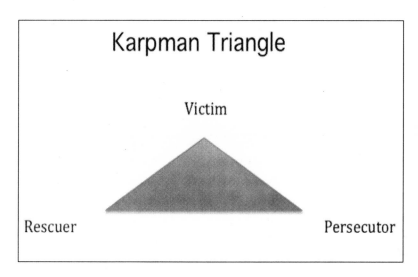

* * *

What we unconsciously seek in the other is the idyllic parenting we did not receive. We secretly hope to get it "right" this time. Falling in love is largely a matter of falling into the illusion that we will finally, fully, and forever get our needs met. Perhaps we visualize a cozy and comfortable existence, much like a warm bath, in which we float contentedly, protected from exposure to unpleasant extremes of temperature or irritating shocks to our systems. Perhaps we imagine a devoted caregiver ministering to our every need as a perfect mother would lovingly and sensitively respond to every passing need of her infant. Or perhaps we project unending admiration and loyal support from our partner, just as our ideal parents would applaud enthusiastically even the most minor accomplishment of their young offspring.

How disillusioning to discover that instead of uninterrupted womb-like bliss, we are pitched into tiresome disagreements and painful conflicts. That instead of being ministered to, we are expected to minister to the incessant needs and demands of the other. That in the place of that unassailable support and validation we expected, we meet the condemning judgments we had hoped to escape. How brutal the shock when instead of the All-Good Mother, we find our Superego embodied in our partner. This person we thought would sweep away the slings and arrows of frustration and disappointment becomes the one who wields the bow. Where I hoped to find Mary Poppins, I find Darth Vader instead.

How often have I heard the same story from couples in therapy. One person laments, "I have to do everything! Without me, s/he would be lost! S/he never helps out or makes plans for anything. I'm always the one in charge. S/he never takes the initiative. It's always up to me."

The other complains: "Nothing I ever do is good enough! It always has to be his/her way! I can never live up to his/her expectations. No one could!"

It seems immediately obvious that a parent/child relationship is operating here. On the surface, the over-functioning spouse commands the parental role. But, deeper still, it will appear from what was said above that the over-functioner also houses a needy child who yearns for parenting. On the deeper level, what we have, in reality, is two children squabbling about who gets to be taken care of. Until we learn to parent ourselves, marriage will be, in essence, a relationship between two adult children fighting not to grow up.

The way out is:

1. Becoming Aware

First and foremost, we must learn to hear the child in ourselves, to recognize the voice and acknowledge the feelings of the child within.

2. Validating

In place of the customary disparagement of the Superego, we must practice consistently responding to ourselves with empathic and legitimizing comments along the lines of "you have a right to feel...", "that's okay," "you deserve to be ..."

3. Advocating

Having validated the feelings of the child, we then determine what would be helpful in the situation, what action needs to be taken to advocate for the child, and what is our responsibility in promoting change.

* * *

I quit comparing myself to my high-energy partner and stopped working night and day. It will be a life-long discipline being responsive to the needs of the child.

* * *

To clarify the process of becoming a sympathetic witness or nurturing parent to the child, I offer some examples, rather like a chorus, of child voices in my clientele.

The Cat Lady

She was small and slight and very pretty. She sat poised on the edge of her chair, leaning eagerly toward me as if she could not wait to hear my next precious thought. Her voice was creamy and sweet, like a bowl of warm milk, and she almost purred when she spoke. She didn't come very often, but when she did, she always had an agenda of one or more problems that she would drop at my feet, hopefully, like a sack of near-drowned kittens I was meant to revivify. What an ego boost when I succeeded in pulling a cat out of the bag! How wizardly-wise I felt!

One day the cat lady came to complain about her sister-in-law, by her account a thoroughly impossible person whom she could barely tolerate. What was most unbearable about her, according to my client, was her appalling lack of honesty. She described in detail incident after incident in which she had mustered all her patience and forbearance to convey to her sister-in-law an impression of loving acceptance, but the woman persisted in her stubborn hypocrisy.

Gradually, it dawned on her that the duplicity she saw in her sister-in-law was a mirror of herself - that the little girl behind the smile was neither patient, sweet, nor nice. When she began to acknowledge her true feelings and drop the loving act, her need for change in her sister-in-law quickly diminished, as did their contact.

Iron Man

His parents split up when he was five and he lived with his mother. He hated his father and was clear he wanted *nothing* to do with him. As a boy, his father had always criticized and disparaged him, calling him a bozo, an idiot, and a "schmeckel-head" who could never do anything right. He had only seen his father once in many years and that was once too many, as far as he was concerned. He did not want to talk about his father or think about his father. He repeated, with insistence, he wanted *nothing* to do with him.

His father was an alcoholic and he himself almost never took a drink out of fear he would be like him. His father was loud and belligerent and he was so afraid to speak up for himself that he was being exploited in his work situation and in his relationship with his brother who lived with (or off) him. He came into therapy because he was sabotaging his training for the Iron Man marathon by cigarette smoking and excessive self-criticism. What plagued him most was his constant dread of being the failure his father had predicted he would be. Behind his wall of anger was a little boy still cowering beneath his father's critical gaze.

One day it came to the surface: the child's deep disappointment, grief and rage. "He was never there for me," he cried. "He always let me down! I wanted him to be the most important person in my life!"

"But he *is*," I whispered softly. "He is." This man he

refused to acknowledge was the pivotal figure in his life.

Mr. Normal

He wore a pin-striped suit and gold rimmed spectacles. He was a business executive, he said, with a tone of casual matter-of-factness. From his crested handkerchief to his polished shoes, he was the ideal image of a corporate business executive. From his carefully modulated voice to his serious-but-open expression, everything about him fit the image, one might almost say, like a Platonic Form. Perhaps it was just this perfection that gave away the act. It was as if beneath his flawless presentation, as if behind his studied nonchalance, an eager young boy peeked out from the far corner of the stage curtain inquiring earnestly: "Well, how am I doing?"

He did it very well. He was motivated and personable and unswervingly professional. He never lost his cool. He was a very high level executive.

Then wasn't it odd that he always feared that he couldn't make the grade? He drank too much, he worked too hard, and he was cheating on his wife. Still, he conducted his affair discreetly, on business trips, after work hours, and with another married executive, taking care to avoid crossing ranks in the company or jeopardizing his role in the family. He was a very classic married executive.

As therapy progressed, it became more and more apparent how thin was his veneer. Inside he housed an insecure child who was desperate for approval. He hid the secret shame of a family that was far from being "normal".

He never knew his father, who had left before his birth, except for the fact that he had a drinking problem that, he surmised, must have been severe. "Without doubt," he mused, "my mother could have driven him to it." He was raised by his mom and grandmother in a tough part of town along with his deaf and dumb aunt who'd had cerebral meningitis and his retarded cousin who had cerebral palsy. "Picture us walking down the street," he remarked ruefully. "Four women and me. What did I know about being a man? Or what did I know about normality?" Deep inside his pin-striped suit, he hid the fear of being a freak.

*   *   *

In each of these cases, we see that the child's voice was blocked because there was an aspect of the child's experience that the adult strove to deny. In the Cat Lady it was her dishonesty, in the Iron Man his need for fathering, in Mr. Normal the fear of being socially unacceptable.

The function of the Superego is to support our denial system and perpetuate the false self. When we succeed in overthrowing the tyranny of the Superego, we are free to be our true selves. What, then, if we discover that the selves we are free to be are selves we do not like? Have we freed ourselves only to turn away from ourselves, again, in disdain?

In the next section, we will explore in depth the process of wrestling with the shadow.

Part Four

Wrestling with the Shadow

Round One: Anger

. . . though there is in every human being a potential Hitler,

there is also, in each one of us, a potential Mother Theresa.

Elizabeth Kubler-Ross

Although some theorists compare the shadow to a reflection cast by the light, wrestling with the shadow is not, one may observe wryly, like strolling down a shady lane on a sunny day. Frankly, it can be a pretty awful experience. You will have your own visions of what "the awfulest-awful" would be: your own Room 101 as in Orwell's *Nineteen Eighty-Four* [30] or your own *Nightmare in the Closet* [31] as in Mayer's children's book on fear. Whatever it is that represents your shadow, you will recognize it by the intensity of the reaction it provokes. Somewhere inside you may feel like screaming:

NOT THAT!   NOT NOW!   NOT ME!

Invariably, it is that which we recoil from in some deep, core way. I call it: "The Great Ick."

While we have our individual variations rooted in our personal histories, there are two universal themes that emerge from what was said before. They can be pictured diagrammatically like this:

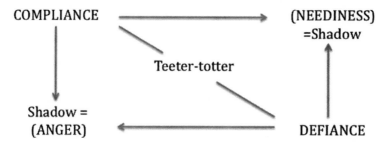

This is the shadow dance of compliance and defiance.

Beginning on the left side of the diagram, the compliant posture presupposes an implicit acceptance of our neediness. It is grounded in recognition of our deep-seated and inescapable needs for physical and emotional caretaking. It constitutes,

30 Orwell, George: *Nineteen Eighty-Four,* first published by Martin Secker & Warburg 1949, later by Penguin Books, London, 1954.
31 Mayer, Mercer: *There's A Nightmare in My Closet,* Dial Books for Young Readers, E.P. Dutton, New York 1968.

in effect, a decision to regard these needs as primary. Who I will be and how I will behave will essentially be legislated by what I believe will gain me love, approval and nurturance. The inclination of compliant people to be accommodating to others is, therefore, a direct consequence of acknowledging our dependence on them. Anything that could jeopardize the fulfillment of our basic dependency needs will be experienced as intrinsically threatening.

In view of this dependence, we do not wish to do anything that might incite withdrawal or rejection by the object of our need. It is a short step from this position to the avoidance of anger altogether, either other people's or our own.

In the inscription to his newly published book on anger, Barry Boeckner says:

"Anger is like fire...it makes a good friend, but a terrible enemy."[32]

Compliant people have no intention of befriending a force as powerful and potentially destructive as anger can be. They want as little as possible to do with it. They try to pretend it does not exist. We can all recognize the person who says, through clenched teeth, "Angry? I'm not angry. Whatever you want is just fine with me."

If anger simply went away, this might be a workable strategy. But it doesn't. It simmers and burns. It creates resentment which smolders and seeps out sidewards poisoning our relationships, or seeps inward poisoning our bodily functioning. Despite our efforts to suppress and repress it, it lives within us. We swallow it and it upsets our digestive systems. We brace ourselves against it and develop pains in our backs and necks. The effort to suppress our anger creates an underlying strain and tension in us. We appear "forced" or rigidly mechanical. Our pleasantness has a hollow ring. All our emotions seem muted and colorless. Not only to others but also to ourselves, there appears to be something "missing",

---

32 Boeckner, Barry: *Angerworks*, Cambridge Interfaith Family Counselling Centre, Cambridge, Ontario, 1993, page 7.

something flat or stale about our lives. We are going through the motions and doing all the right things. But the passion is gone — or the sense of meaning.

Full-scale denial of anger produces what Jane Goldberg terms "the *Pathological Niceness Syndrome:*"

> People suffering from this syndrome have as their paramount goal the avoidance of anger and of being disliked. They strive not to feel anger, and they strive even more strenuously not to have others feel angry toward them. They repress all feelings of hostility, envy, competitiveness, jealousy, and resentment. Yet, without these "negative" feelings, a person becomes compliant, passive, selfless, and overly anxious to please - in short, a miserable shadow of a person. [33]

Alternatively, our pattern might be to go along agreeably until, one day, we just explode. We have a fit of anger, then feel guilty, and hastily return to our customary submissiveness. We are contrite; we act remorseful. We try to make amends until, inevitably as time passes, the explosion erupts again.

In the passive-aggressive style of operating, we appear agreeable on the surface while, beyond our awareness, resistance gathers force underground. Despite our best intentions, when the time comes for action, "something" always intervenes. We forgot; we tried; we couldn't help it; it wasn't our fault, we say. There is always a good reason why our promises are broken and our agreements unfulfilled. However elaborate and convincing our attempts at vindication, do we ever wonder why we so often feel misunderstood and unjustly blamed?

The truth is, we are in denial. It is more than mere coincidence that the partner of a passive-aggressive person will invariably be enraged. Even when they can't punch holes in our rationalizations, what infuriates the other is their perpetual experience of being let down. What our partners know, though we deny, is that whenever they depend on us, it is absolutely predictable that *something* will go wrong. While

33 Goldberg, Jane: *The Dark Side of Love*, G. P. Putman's Sons, New York, 1993, page 47.

the pattern remains invisible, our denial drives them wild. In the helpless rage of the other, it is as if we hear an echo of the anger we've disowned.

As we treat anger, so we will treat all the other negative emotions we are not supposed to feel. By disowning the scurrilous members of this family, do we presume we can be free of being tainted by them? Probably the most difficult emotion for us to accept, the most outcast and vilified, is hatred. "We have become," as Goldberg says, "a society that hates hate." [34]

In envisioning ourselves as decent, moral, loving individuals, we will declare that hate has no place in our hearts. We may, at best, admit to passing anger, even rage, at our loved ones, but we will   vehemently deny the possibility that we might actually hate them even as we love them. Of all human emotions, hate seems to be the most reviled.[35]

Hatred, spite, envy, malice, desire for revenge - these are all anathema to the peace-loving, compliant type. We not only refuse to express such feelings; we also refuse to feel them. We simply disavow their existence. They become foreign to our picture of ourselves. In order to uphold an image of ourselves as moral, decent, virtuous and nice, we would far rather get ulcers than give them.

Thus, as we see in the diagram above, neediness is the implicit ally of compliance while anger (and its family of negative emotions) is its shadow and is consciously disowned.

On the other side of the teeter-totter, the logical opposite and invariable complement to compliance is the posture of defiance. And whereas compliance is repelled by anger and runs the other way, defiance cozies up with it and makes itself at home. The raging tyrant, the bombastic drill sergeant, and the storming Rambo are all examples of the hot anger employed by defiant types.

---

34 Ibid., page 6.
35 Ibid., page 4.

But there is also a cold anger, which, though quieter, is no less potent and intimidating than the hot variety. It takes the form of stony silence, a cold disapproving look, or a cutting remark. It may use exclusion, withholding, or unresponsiveness to drive its point home. But the steely coldness of its rage is unmistakable. It is an anger that can freeze us in our tracks, fling us out into the cold, or chill us to the bone. Cruelty is portrayed as "cold" and harsh criticism "cuts like ice," we say.

Whether hot or cold, the anger of defiance is a blast of power intended to impress, suppress, or dominate the other. The message is: you'd better listen *or else...*

Or else **what?** Forcing the issue exposes the brinkmanship inherent in the message of defiance. What the defiant cannot face is the *what*. Threats of abandonment and rejection are flung out with great gusto and an air of supreme unconcern. In actuality, this is bravado. Like the cowardly lion, we conceal our fear behind an exaggeratedly ferocious roar.

The secret that cowers behind this haughty display of power is a terror of our own vulnerability. Force the hand of a defiant and you will observe its empty bluster fizzle out. It is precisely because of a deep-seated fear of dependence that we adopt the defiant posture as a show of force. We are trying to convince others - and, even more, ourselves - that we are strong, powerful and in control. For this reason, we occupy rigid and uncompromising positions. We demand to have our way. We won't budge since, after all, we think: "who needs you anyway?" The answer "we do" is forcibly suppressed. What is denied, often adamantly, in the defiant posture is our neediness.

Thus, the logic is complete. Each opposite accepts and operates on what the other disowns. While compliance readily acknowledges the neediness abhorred by defiance, defiance readily harnesses the anger that compliance actively avoids. It becomes apparent that where these two meet, the sparks will fly.

The drama escalates as we recall that these opposites are always paired. One implies the other. Where one is present, the other is always presupposed. Each manifests for the other the shadow of itself. They are intimate partners, born in conflict, whose task it is to come to terms with each other. It is not possible, therefore, to deal with one without dealing with them both. One could say that the shadow is a two-headed beast.

To wrestle with the shadow will mean, therefore, coming to terms with both aspects of ourselves: the anger disowned by compliance and the neediness disowned by defiance. We must be prepared to contend with the turbulent ups and downs of this interior see saw.

*   *   *

When I went into Gestalt therapy training, I was the picture of compliance, a preppie in a counter-culture world. I wanted to please but the rules made pleasing unacceptable. I was caught in a classic double-bind. To gain approval, I had to give up seeking approval. My compliance had to go underground. "I am not in this world to live up to your expectations," declared the Gestalt prayer. Or if I am, I better not appear to be.

Paradoxically, the expectation was to act as if there were no expectations. "Be yourself" was the watchword of the faith. While there is nothing wrong with this motto when we understand its meaning, it provides no guideline for a compliant type to use. What was my "self" and when was I being it? What was truly me and what was not? When was I genuine and when was I merely playing at being genuine as befit the budding Gestalt therapist role? The truth is, I had no idea. So I hid. I said little, I melted into the background and, inwardly, I shook.

What made matters worse was that the primary coping mechanisms I had developed to negotiate my way in the world were denigrated here. (More than a hint of the schizoid double-bind: "Be yourself— but be what we want you to be.")

I was an intellectual with a capital "I". I had always analyzed my way through life. I used logic to interpret people and relationships, and I knew it wasn't working for me. What had brought me to Gestalt training was the inescapable conclusion that the logical apparatus I had perfected as a Philosophy professor had proved dismally inadequate to address the turmoil of my life. I had chosen Gestalt therapy as the direct antithesis of Philosophy in being focused exclusively on feeling rather than on thought. "Lose your head and come to your senses," Perls[36] had said. And I was taught in no uncertain terms that analyzing and rationalizing, as I was wont to do, were not permissible. Hour after hour, we were drilled in grueling awareness exercises designed to force us out of our heads. But my head was the only safe place I knew. So I hid.

The evaluation I received at the end of my first year of training was that I was "like a squirrel." I stuck my head out only occasionally and then, they said, I would promptly run back into my burrow. They were right. The world I experienced out there was not a safe place to be.

By the end of my second year of training, I had a radically different evaluation. They said I was "like a fishwife" and, they added reprovingly, I was not as smart as I appeared to be. From squirrel to fishwife in one short year?!? What had happened to me?

I believe now that I had taken a ride on the teeter-totter. In place of my customary compliance, I had learned to substitute defiance as a mode of being in the world. Was it mere coincidence that all the women in our Gestalt training group learned to turn their tears into anger while all the men learned to turn their anger into tears?

After two years of training, I no longer dissolved into a puddle when someone was angry with me. I learned to rally and shout back with the best of them.

But, again, they were right if their reproach was meant to

---

36 For a presentation of Gestalt therapy in action, see Perls, Frederick: *Gestalt Therapy Verbatim*, Bantam Books, New York , 1969.

indicate that defiance was no less a posture, no more genuine, than · my previous compliance had been. It was refreshing - one might say, empowering - to have a choice of defensive styles in place of being locked into the same old one, so long as it is clear that they are equally within the realm of the false self.

To move beyond the false self would ultimately mean getting off the teeter-totter altogether.

*   *   *

Wrestling with the shadow means dancing with it first. It means embracing the part of us we have turned away from, the part we have resolutely shunned.

The shadow we will first engage is the rage and hatred underlying niceness in human beings and our consequent potential for evil and destruction.

Compliants would like to pretend that good and evil are entirely separate and that good can exist without evil, particularly in us. I believe this view is fundamentally mistaken. The position I take, though it may appear to be unsavory, pessimistic or unflattering, is nonetheless unequivocal. It says:

(1) Rage and hatred are both natural elements in the human psyche and inevitable accompaniments to caring and love in human relationships.

(2) Rage and hatred *may* give rise to destructive acts but they need not. Whether or not evil results from rage and hatred is a function of our awareness and our choice of action.

(3) Acknowledging our rage and hatred is a definite benefit to our psychological and physical health so long as we can learn to accept these feelings without acting them out. They are essential aspects of our being without which we cannot be whole.

In this point of view, I join company with Freud, Winnicott, Goldberg, and a few stalwart others. It is a position that runs directly counter to our prevailing way of viewing ourselves and one that we strenuously resist.

This difference of opinion is more than just a theoretical debate. The vision we hold of what it is to be human profoundly affects the way we perceive and evaluate both ourselves and others with whom we are in relationship. This vision, largely unexamined, often inarticulate, is, nonetheless, the basis on which we will feel either self-condemning or self-accepting, sternly judgmental of others or calmly tolerant and compassionate. It is a vision that is *lived*. Therefore, how we think and feel about this issue is critical.

While the general consensus of opinion is directly opposed to this position, a more "enlightened" minority might agree. Those of us who have, for instance, attended an anger workshop or read some key self-help book from Rubin [37] to Bach [38] to Birnbaum [39] may presume to know better. At least, we pay lip service to the view that anger and its expression are healthy.

But how do we, in fact, operate? Do we practice what we preach? Does our anger come out cleanly and appropriately in all situations or do we err in the direction of implosion or explosion? Do we feel guilty or remorseful in either case?

On an even deeper level, whether we desist from expressing anger or spew it out with vigor, do we inwardly berate ourselves for feeling angry at all? Do we silently condemn others for having rageful feelings and, perhaps, lose our sense of trust or comfort with those who are angry towards us?

Whatever our intellectual position, as we live our lives, is anger actually welcomed or feared? And if, by chance, anger passes the acid test, what about hatred? Will it pass too? Or

37 Rubin, Theodore Isaac: *The Angry Book*, Collier Books, New York, 1970.
38 Bach, George and Wyden, Peter: *The Intimate Enemy*, Avon Books, New York, 1968 and Bach, George and Goldberg, Herbert: *Creative Aggression*, Anchor Doubleday, Garden City, New York, 1983.
39 Birnbaum, Jack: *Cry Anger: A Cure for Depression*, General Publishing, Don Mills, Ontario, 1973.

is hatred, as in the classic joke about discrimination, like a suitor of a certain color, class or religion whom we profess to tolerate, while secretly confiding, "I wouldn't let **my** daughter marry one."

I myself, a certified product of Gestalt training, argued doggedly for the open and direct expression of anger in the face of fierce resistance from my mate. On the cognitive level, I was an unassailable defender of the faith. I believed in what I said, but living this belief was something else again.

On the emotional level, his unremitting criticism hurt. Imperceptibly, my staunch belief began to crumble and self-doubt reared its head. Bit by bit, I slid away from my own conviction until a voice inside was echoing *him*. Inexorably it repeated: "There must be something *wrong* with me for me to be so angry!"

As we explore the arguments concerning rage and hatred, it will be important to be open to *both* levels of yourself - the cognitive *and* the emotional. Whether you locate yourself in the majority or the minority camp, you will need to examine how you think about the dark side of humankind, as well as how your thinking gets embodied in the actual practice of your life.

At first glance, an idealistic view of human beings may appear to be intrinsically more appealing than one that sees our angelic and demonic sides in balance. At least *prima facie*, the former accords us a more flattering moral status and paints us in a rosier light. Our egos are not eager to concede that people are as given to being hateful and destructive as they are to being loving and kind. Cheery optimism seems by far the favored choice.

But the reality is, as we discovered before[40], that the attempt to live up to idealistic standards of perfection generates hatred of self while the same expectation projected on others generates hatred of them. Conversely, when we expect less of ourselves and others, when we are in touch with our human defects and

40 cf. above, Part One, page 31

flaws, we are more inclined to be tolerant and compassionate. In this paradoxical twist, the more we acknowledge hating, the more loving we will be.

If we insist on a picture of ourselves as totally benevolent and kind-hearted beings who never experience hatred and rage, we will have to perform some sort of "radical surgery" on our psyches when they confront us with contradictory evidence, as inevitably they will.

To maintain our Pollyanna picture, we will have to force these unwelcome experiences out of our awareness, utilizing any of the following psychosurgical procedures that will banish them from view.

Depression is one frequently utilized method of converting anger we feel toward others into anger we direct toward the self. Then, by a kind of inner contracting, we succeed in squeezing the energy out of this anger until all that remains is a perpetual gloominess, a flat greyness, a dark hopelessness that dogs us, day in day out.

Projection is another common method of obliterating our anger toward others by turning it outward rather than inward and attributing it to the other rather than owning it oneself. Hence, in *paranoid* projection, the intensity of our fear of others directly reflects the intensity of the hatred we project on others and then experience as directed against ourselves.

If our anger is not yet buried through depression or projection, we can use *somatizing* to convert it into physical symptoms from minor aches and pains to major ailments and disease. The connection between repression of anger and bodily conditions such as gastric disorders, headaches, muscle spasms, high blood pressure and heart problems is well documented in a new domain of research called psycho-neuro-immunology. The message is clear. Our anger, taken inside, can literally make us sick.

Alternatively, we may attempt to cover up our anger or numb it out through alcohol or drug abuse, or other forms of *addictive* behavior such as compulsive shopping, gambling and eating disorders. If our diseases don't kill us, perhaps our addictive life styles will.

On a collective level, we *rationalize* our anger and aggression by inventing lofty ideological excuses to kill one another with impunity. History is nothing less than a story of war. We repackage vicious feelings as permissible on the grounds that "this is one of *Them*, not one of *Us*."" In place of seeing people like ourselves, we see "the enemy." We use *objectification* to distance ourselves from others and dehumanize the objects of our violence.

Fusion allows us to reach the same conclusion from the opposite approach: that is, it mitigates our awareness of their otherness. We treat others as if they were a part of us or belonged to us, like material possessions, in much the way that women and children were once regarded by law to be.

If we have the courage to abandon these defensive maneuvers and face the truth of our experience, anger and hate are unmistakable. Yet we need not recoil in guilt or shame unless we hold to the assumption that these are feelings that *should not* be, that they are somehow abnormal, aberrant, or unnatural. If we accept the reality of our experience, it is evident that these dark feelings are, on the contrary, normal, natural, and inevitable. They are a part of what being human means. We might do well to meditate on Jesus' words:

> "If any man come to me, and hate not his father, and mother,
> and wife, and children, and brethren, and sisters, yea, and
> his own life also, he cannot be my disciple."
>
> Luke 14:26

Yet how reluctant we are to embrace this truth. How tenaciously we cling to our childish pictures and refuse to face, in Goldberg's phrase, "the dark side of love."

* * *

I tried so hard to be moral, to play by the rules. I should have been a Girl Guide; I was such a good girl. I always kept my promises. I dared not tell a lie. I was dutiful and conscientious. I tried to follow the Golden Rule. I thought I had to, to be fair.

Even when my mate protested: "Fair? What's fair? Life's not fair", I never questioned my conviction that fairness was the rule. When he shouted at me, "I don't give a ---- about being fair or decent!" I could not take in his words. I stood there open-mouthed and stupefied. And I remained in shell shock as he proved relentlessly that he meant every word. He said, "I'm sorry, I love you," as he turned the legal screws. "I'm sorry, I love you" were his final words to me. "He loves me, he loves me" I kept repeating, like a mantra, as reality rolled over me.

And I persisted in my love for him, no matter what he did. It was uncontrollable and inconsolable, a love without reprieve. I found it infinitely easier to forgive him than it was to forgive me. All who cared for me hated him, with the notable exception of me.

I was wretched. I was intractable. I clung to my love for him and it clung to me.

Then one night I cracked. The anger broke free.

Crack! went the armor of fairness and decency.

Crack! like my naive assumptions that the man I loved and the man I knew would not be dishonest, at least to me, and would never hit a woman, least of all me.

Crack! like my ribs when he finally admitted, after hours of insisting there was nothing to tell that, in fact, he had cheated on me.

Crack! like my skull hitting the cement, twice in a row, when he threw me down and afterward insisted that he didn't know it had.

Crack! as the hate broke out and the witch broke free!

Crack! like the cracking of bones as she broke his beautiful body in two, three, or more pieces and smashed his skull - in fantasy.

Cackle! as the witch spun around and hurled her venom at all those others. The tyrannical father who ruled with fear, the mother consumed in self-pity, the brother who cruelly picked on me, and the sister who wasn't a sister. Any who had ever done me wrong she clawed and ravaged with her fury.

Crackle! as the flames leapt and the sparks flew and the witch hissed and whirled about feverishly.

Rage, long denied, burned free that night, wreaking its revenge. Like liquid fire, it surged through me: sweet, hot and delicious. I tasted the flames and power of that rage coursing through my body. I danced and screeched and laughed and howled as its energy shot through me. The witch and I danced as one in a wild and rapturous frenzy.

For how many years had I been estranged from this fierce life energy. Subdued and depressed, my compliant self was studious, well-behaved, and quiet. I did not suspect that behind that polished law-abidingness, there lay a murderous rage.

Through all those years of slow despair, that savage hatred simmered. From time to time, it bubbled up in volcanic-style eruptions which were quickly doused by the Superego in guilty self-recrimination. But the fiery heart of that hate burned on as a dark suicidal yearning.

Now, with the Superego muzzled, I was free at last to meet and embrace the shadow in me: the hatred, rage and malice I had never been able to see. Finally, I could step out from behind the screen. The wicked witch of the west was: **Me!**

* * *

"Oh, great!" exclaims the Superego disdainfully. "Now we can all go about hacking each other to pieces in the name of wholeness! Lets give our rage and hatred unbridled expression so that we can call ourselves authentic! Just imagine where this will lead!"

As soon as the claim is made that hate and anger are natural, even healthy, it conjures up visions of therapy-crazed individuals out releasing their negative feelings in unrestrained acts of violence. It will be decried as a justification for flagrant abuse of all sorts.

This inference is not only unpalatable but, at the same time. it is totally invalid. It rests on a failure to make the fundamental distinction between *acknowledging* feelings and *acting* them *out* or, as Goldberg puts it, "between the *feeling* of hate and the *use* of the feeling." [41]

> Hate is destructive only when it is translated into destructive behavior. Destructiveness can arise from hate, but it is not an inevitability.
>
> We believe that hate cannot be contained - that once we set a match to our hateful feelings the resulting flames will rage out of control. In fact, just the opposite occurs. It is precisely when we don't allow ourselves to acknowledge our hateful feelings that they gather more destructive potential. [42]

The last point is critical. It is not just that the awareness and acceptance of anger and hate *need* not lead to destructive acts but that such destructive acts are *less* likely to occur if we cultivate awareness and acceptance of these feelings. As Jung [43] argued, it is not the existence of the shadow which leads to evil and destruction but our turning away from it.

In the same vein, M. Scott Peck says: "the central defect of the evil is not the sin but the refusal to acknowledge it." [44] In his psychology of evil, Peck argues that it is the need to maintain a pure and blameless image, as if one were beyond reproach, that characterizes those he would regard as evil.

> Utterly dedicated to preserving their self-image of perfection, they are unceasingly engaged in the effort to

41 Goldberg, Jane: *The Dark Side of Love*, page 45.
42 Ibid., page 45.
43 *Collected Works of C.G. Jung*, Pantheon Books, New York, 1954.
44 Peck, M. Scott: *People of the Lie*, Simon & Schuster Inc., New York, 1983, page 69.

maintain the appearance of moral purity... Their"goodness"
is all on a level of pretense. It is, in effect, a lie. That is why
they are "the people of the lie." Actually, the lie is designed
not so much to deceive others as to deceive themselves.
They cannot or will not tolerate the pain of self-reproach. [45]

In short, for Peck, "we become evil by attempting to hide
from ourselves. [46]

Recognizing anger and hatred as natural components of
being human is, for most of us, an enormous relief. It obviates
the need for pretense, repression and self-castigation when
we discover that everyone has the same dark feelings hidden
within.

But it is more than a relief. It is also our protection
from the sudden explosion of these bottled-up feelings into
aggressive action or, at the other end of the spectrum, the cold
pre-meditated aggression which is rationalized as acceptable
or even as "for one's own good." The less need we have to
deny who we are and how we truly feel, the less need we have
to act it out malevolently.

*   *   *

*My sister always was the funny one. She had a caustic sense
of humor and could make a joke out of anything. She even made
us laugh at my father's funeral, to my eternal shame and chagrin.
We sat in the front row shaking uncontrollably and I prayed that
the people filing in behind us would think we shook with tears. But
I knew better.*

*Some time after the funeral, during the period of mourning, my
mother was waiting for an elevator with a 'babushka' on her head,
worrying about how she looked - a perpetual matter of concern to
her even at such a time. My sister reassured her sweetly. "Don't
worry, Mom, you look fine." Then out shot one of her notorious
one-liners that would be quoted again and again: "Can you come
to me on Fridays?"*

45 Ibid., page 75
46 Ibid., page 76.

When I was in crisis after my mate deserted, I asked for her support. Would she call me please? Would she check up and see how I was doing?

I guess I should have known better. My sister never phoned. It was two and a half years later when she finally called to chat.

"I have no agenda for this phone call," she announced breezily. "It's the new year and I was just thinking of you." Obviously she expected me to play the accommodating role I had always played before. She didn't know the witch was out.

In response to my mention of the rather long delay, she explained that I had not seemed "logical" or "reasonable" to her when I had phoned her more than two years ago. "So what was the point of talking to you?" she asked.

"Were you logical and reasonable when you had your nervous breakdown?" I reminded her. "But I called you anyway."

"I'm sorry I couldn't support you as you wanted, but..." she in turn reminded me, chidingly, "we are still family."

And then she said something aphoristic that my memory has lost about how people need their family. At that moment, I remembered a brochure from a family therapy center that announced boldly: "A family is a circle of people who love you." I certainly didn't have that.

"I don't have a family," the witch spoke up. "And the only thing I need from you now is information."

She repeated my words incredulously. Then she replied curtly: "If you need information, dial 4-1-1."

My sister always was the funny one.

* * *

What is positive about anger and hate? Again, the Superego will be skeptical because it speaks as the proponent of civilized life, which, as Freud[47] argued, is based on the repression and sublimation of our more aggressive natures. Yet aggressive impulses are not bad in themselves. They are

---

47 Freud, Sigmund: *Civilization and Its Discontents*, (translated by James Strachey), W.W. Norton & Co. Inc., New York, 1961.

fundamental to survival.

Anger is an announcement by the body that something is *not* okay. I compare it to a smoke detector. Like anger, a smoke detector gives us warning of a possible threat. We need the qualifier "possible" because, admittedly, errors do occur. We do misinterpret and misperceive and imagine threats in situations where there are none.

In my home, the smoke detector went off every time I used the broiler in my oven. But I did not, for that reason, decide to disconnect it since, one of those times, it just might have been a fire after all. Obviously, it made more sense to make a judgment call on each occasion than to forfeit my warning system altogether. Just so, with anger, we may not choose to act on our angry feelings every time we feel them, but we will certainly want to have the opportunity to make that decision for ourselves.

Anger is an energy for change. It mobilizes action. On the most basic level, it gives rise to a "fight or flight" reaction. Without this energy, our will is weak. We remain paralyzed and frozen. Often victims will spend years in an abusive relationship because they cannot summon up the energy for change. They do not realize that they may have a need to get angry.

Anger is involvement. It says: Pay attention. This is important. I care about this. This affects me. I am not indifferent. Anger is a mode of being *in relation*.

Anger has complex ties to hurt, to fear, and to impotence. Perhaps it needs to stand aside sometimes so that we can see what is beside or beneath it. But it is a mistake, I think, for us to reduce it, analyze it, or reframe it out of existence. Anger is our strength to stand up and protect ourselves. Though it can be misused, it is a force for life.

Some people see hatred as an extreme form of anger, while others distinguish anger and hate, regarding them as fundamentally different. It may be said that anger is a desire to *connect* - to make an impact, to change, even to hurt the other - whereas hatred seems to be a desire to *disconnect* from the other, to have *less* of the other, or, in the extreme, to obliterate the other altogether.

By disconnecting self from other, hatred puts a boundary around the self and differentiates self from other. It is a movement toward separation, away from fusion, in the direction of self-identity. Thus, hatred can help us define ourselves. On this point, Goldberg says:

> Hate, sometimes manifest as the desire for the death of a loved one, is often the only means we have of separating ourselves from others. Fantasies of a loved one's death serve as compensation for a relationship in which the lives and minds of two people are too closely intertwined. Hate is a sign that there is a striving toward individual development. It is a natural by-product of a healthy process. [48]

Hate encourages independence. We are less likely to become enmeshed in a fused relationship if we have a healthy dose of hatred at our psychological disposal. This means that denial of hateful feelings in a family can actually prove damaging to the development of a sense of self.

> The mother who does not permit herself to hate her child is refusing to respond to the real person that child is. In such an atmosphere of denial, the child will never have the feeling that he is known, accepted, and fully loved for who he is. [49]

Goldberg echoes psychoanalyst Donald Winnicott who states:

> It seems to me doubtful whether a human child, as he develops, is capable of tolerating the full extent of his own hate in a sentimental environment. He needs hate to hate. [50]

---

48 Goldberg, Jane: *The Dark Side of Love*, page 47.
49 Ibid., page 57.
50 quoted in *The Dark Side of Love*, page 58.

* * *

One night when we were out to dinner, my mother let loose her hate and rage at me. I don't recall the details of her attack but the climaxing statement is indelibly carved in my memory.

"I am cutting the umbilical cord!" she hissed at me. The umbilical cord?? I didn't know if I should laugh or cry. I was thirty-six years old and she was just contemplating cutting the cord to me!

The last gift I received from my mother was a box of debris. She had sent two framed photographs of her parents, whom I never knew and felt no connection to, by mail in a soft cardboard box. They arrived with the glass shattered, the frames chipped, and the photographs scratched and cut.

She also enclosed a photograph of me, one that was her favorite and that had been displayed in the living room for years. It was a particularly melancholy shot and it struck me that the twenty-three year old girl in the photo looked extremely depressed.

There was a scrap of white paper in the box with a note in my mother's handwriting, addressed to nobody, and unsigned. "Thought you'd like to have this" was all it said.

* * *

Hatred clears away obstruction. It can penetrate the mystification that entraps us and dissolve illusion. It can be a force for truth. When we feel as if we want to destroy ourselves or other people, there is a dim perception that something false needs to be removed.

But we are in danger of throwing out the baby with the bath water. Instead of eliminating the repressive and abusive aspects of ourselves that stand in the way of our being whole, we may believe we need to abolish the self in its entirety. Suicidal and murderous feelings are a resounding message that something has to die. But it is not the human being but the *way* of being that needs to go. These feelings are alarm bells to be attended to, not acted out. The hate that impels them is our guide to what is poisoning our lives if we have the wisdom to understand its guidance. It can kill and it can heal. Hatred is strong medicine.

Before we leave off examining our preconceptions about hatred, I want to peer into one more shadowy and unexplored vision, not to be dismissed as wholly tongue in cheek, which I entitle:

Sympathy for the Witch

No one talks about the fact that the wicked witch of the west lost her sister. On its descent into Oz, Dorothy's house landed on top of her and she was killed. We forget about that.

There is no sympathy for the wicked witch in the story, even though she has good reason to be upset. She is black with grief and outrage and she wants revenge for her sister's death. In another movie, she might have been a hero and have been revered. No doubt, this would be more likely if she had she been a man.

One can see that, from Dorothy's point of view, the killing clearly was an accident. It's not as though she had any control over her house as it went careening through space. But it would be hard to expect a woman of such extensive power as the witch to simply accept her fate and succumb to helplessness. She has to act. How is she to avenge her sister's death? Is she to blame the house or the tornado or nature or just blind chance? If there is to be someone to blame, who else is there to pick? Dorothy, the intruder, the alien, is the obvious choice.

We could say that Dorothy herself is a recent trauma survivor, having just been swept up by a tornado and deposited in a foreign land. So the witch blames someone who, like her sister and like herself, is a victim of tragic circumstance.

One might conclude that, as a grief reaction to the loss of her sister, the witch has legitimate anger that she does not have the ability to contain. However, she was clearly identified as "wicked" before this tragedy occurred and was already viewed with deep fear and suspicion by the Munchkins. Probably her sister was her only ally in an unreceptive world. We must concede that she possessed a less than charming and endearing style of approach, but there is probably an explanation in her history and good reason for her hostile personality. Maybe, we could hypothesize, it was because her mother was a witch.

Or could she be, in effect, the scapegoat or the identified patient in a dysfunctional system? How do we know that she is bad? Is it possible that we are blindly swallowing a local popular myth by assuming she is, as the Munchkins say, a "wicked" witch? Can we be certain we are not being co-opted if we endorse without question the rightness of these apparently innocent little folk?

And how about this so-called "good" witch named Galinda? Is she the wicked witch's sister too? Is it self-evident that Galinda is to be trusted? Is everyone who arrives in a bubble and has a sweet voice necessarily honest and pure?

What about the morality of breaking into someone's castle for the purpose of stealing their broom? Isn't this a B and E with Theft? How about when Dorothy douses the witch and she melts? Does the fact that she is known as "a witch," or even "a wicked witch," make it morally acceptable to kill her? Even if Dorothy did not suspect what would happen when she threw the water, shouldn't this be a Manslaughter charge at best?

It is vitally important to question our preconceptions about witches. Otherwise, we might find ourselves hanging out with the brainless, the heartless and the gutless, a long way from home.

*   *   *

Contrary to our usual preconceptions, the admission of hateful feelings in ourselves and in our loved ones turns out to facilitate healthy individuation and the development of self-acceptance, as well as acceptance of the uniqueness of each other. In this way hate, managed constructively, can be seen to contribute to the establishment of respectful boundaries, rather than the violation we generally anticipate.

The startling conclusion is that hate is not the arch-enemy

of love that we have supposed it to be, but in a deep, powerful sense, its ally. To love ourselves, we need to learn to love our hate.

Once we overcome the Superego-style objections to acknowledging angry and hateful feelings, what are we to do with them? What is the middle ground between denial and discharge, between disowning and acting out?

There are two possibilities that allow us to release negative feelings without hurting anyone: they are *fantasy* and *talking about*. Let us look at each in turn.

Fantasy is the realm of the *as if*. It is the world of imagination, the spontaneous play land of the child, where we can freely explore possibilities and express feelings without any destructive impact in reality. In general, the freer we are to fantasize, the less likely we will be to act out.

I will run through a quick smorgasbord of favorite fantasy exercises which I have found helpful in exorcising angry feelings. You can try them out yourself and determine what works best for you. For this experiment, just think of someone who brings up the witch (or whatever is the diabolical equivalent) in you.

1. *Hit them out*

The tried-and-true method of releasing angry feelings is to assume a kneeling position and punch a pillow or lie down on a mattress and hit with your arms and kick with your feet. If you are lying on your back, you will have maximum range of movement. However, some people prefer to lie on their stomachs and scream into a pillow to muffle the noise.

It is helpful to begin with non-verbal sounds such as grunts, groans, screams, and roars, and then allow words - often expletives - to emerge as they seem to fit. You can also work with a plastic bat, available in children's toy departments at a very inexpensive price, or the soft stuffed bats called "batakas," which can also be used for two-person fights.

What these hitting methods have in common is their direct way of releasing the tension that builds up in the musculature when we are angry. It is far better for the healthy functioning of our bodies if we can "get it out." Somatic methods such as these work best, however, if we combine them with visualization and imagine the person we are angry at when we hit. Though perfectly obvious, we may frequently need to remind ourselves that pillows, mattresses, and the absent targets of our anger are feeling no pain as we strike.

2. Silent abreaction

Many of us have deep-seated objections to releasing our anger through physical modes of expression, even if we realize how beneficial that would be, or we may find ourselves in situations which are not conducive to this highly energetic style of release. Fortunately, there is a quiet armchair method called "silent abreaction" developed by a leading hypnotherapist, Helen Watkins,[51] which adapts remarkably well to this use. It requires, however, that you know how to induce self-hypnosis or, at least, to put yourself into a deeply relaxed state of mind. This knowledge is readily available through a wide array of resources that offer training in self-hypnosis, meditation and/ or relaxation and is so helpful to your health and well being that I have no hesitation in recommending it as a gift to yourself.

In the ideal circumstance, the first session of silent abreaction would be guided by a trained hypnotherapist and, hopefully, by someone whom you trust. However, you do not need the Cadillac version to get substantial benefit from using this method by yourself. My version of silent abreaction proceeds as follows:

When you are in a hypnotic or deeply relaxed state, imagine that you are walking through the woods on a lovely day in your favorite season of the year. Fill in all the details of

---

51 Watkins, Helen H.: "The Silent Abreaction", *The International Journal of Clinical and Experimental Hypnosis*, 1980, Vol. XXVIII, No. 2, pages 101-113.

the scenery using visual, auditory, and kinesthetic cues. E.g. What do you see around you? What are the colors? sizes? shapes? What is the quality of the light? What sounds do you hear? What is the temperature of the air on your skin? What sensations do you experience in your body? How do you feel inside and out? Continue attending to and expanding on the details until the experience is vivid and you are present in it.

Then imagine that you round a bend and find a large boulder blocking the path. Notice its size and shape. This boulder will represent the anger that is in your way. The size of the boulder will be a handy diagnostic tool for the extent of your anger as you begin your work, as well as of your progress as the work proceeds. Do not make any conscious effort to control the size of the boulder; simply observe what arises spontaneously.

Your work will be to hit the boulder as *hard* as you can for as *long* as you can and to keep on hitting until you are completely satiated. Beside the boulder on the ground you will find a variety of tools that will be available for use in demolishing the boulder such as: a sledgehammer, a club, a wedge, a pick, sticks of dynamite, etc. Choose some tool or tools and start hitting the boulder as hard as you can. You should imagine a voice in the background urging you on with support and encouragement. It will say things like: "Hit that boulder! That's right! You can do it! Keep on! Harder! Even harder! Good for you! Keep it up!" (Your guide, if you have one, will play this role for you.)

When you have done all you can to destroy the boulder, notice what has happened to it. What condition is it in? Is it damaged? How much is broken? What form does the damage take? How much is left intact? Answers to these questions will offer more diagnostic detail. But, for now, just notice; don't dwell on this.

Nearby is a grassy knoll in a little clearing in the woods. Take yourself there now and lie down on the velvety soft ground. Breathe deeply. Gaze up at the azure blue sky and feel your body sink into a deeply relaxed state. Rest and enjoy the comfort after all that exertion. Let your body sink into the soft ground.

Feel a wave of pleasure and well being moving up your body from your toes and feet up to your knees. As the wave reaches your knees, think of something positive about yourself, something that you admire about yourself as a person. Now feel the wave of well being move from your knees up to your chest. Let yourself know that this wave of pleasure is a wave of power, your power. Again think of something positive about you as a person and tell this to yourself. Then let the wave move from your chest to the top of your head until your whole body is bathed in warm, tingling pleasure. This is your power. Enjoy it. Feel it radiating through every part of your body. Tell yourself what a wonderful person you are and congratulate yourself on the anger you have just released.

You can do silent abreaction on a regular basis until you experience the power to overcome any obstacle on your path and any pent-up anger is reduced. Be sure to enjoy the stroll in the woods until the next boulder in your life appears.

3. Chew them out

Perhaps you are in a situation where, at this moment, you simply cannot lie down and hit a pillow or a boulder, even in imagination. For instance, a client of mine worked in an office every day with a man who drove her wild with rage. He bent her roses, hid her desk supplies, and wrote her nasty and belligerent notes. She needed an on-the-spot, on-going methodology to deal with her anger (at least until she got up the nerve to quit). I suggested she *chew him up*.

Like the animals we have evolved from, much of our anger is held in the jaw. We clench our teeth or grind them. We bar our teeth or show our fangs. We have many expressions in our language for the aggressive use of our mouths and teeth. E.g.

"He bit my head off; she chewed me out; he gave me a tongue-lashing; she took a bite out of me". Ripping, tearing, and grinding movements of our teeth are a natural way to express aggression, as anyone who is angry and turns to compulsive eating may demonstrate.

Therefore, chewing gum and imagining we are chewing up someone we are angry at is a very effective strategy, as is fantasizing that we are eating someone up. Despite our initial remonstrations against such a procedure, the more graphic and vivid the fantasy, the better. Give yourself permission to bite their arms, legs, heads and faces in imagination. Be very specific. Experience the taste and texture of that person as you chew. Are they bitter? tough? or mushy? Can you eat them all up? You may even notice that some people are hard to digest!

If the Superego objects that such a method is savage, repulsive, or discourteous, remember: we are less likely to be verbally abusive to other people and "chew them out" with our words if we are free to do so in our fantasy.

4. Write them out

An equally classic and bona fide method of releasing negative feelings is to write them out. For some of us, the pen is mightier than the pillow or the jaw as a mode of expressing angry feelings (or, for that matter, any other type).

Writing interweaves uncovering, discovering, and surfacing feelings with formulating, articulating, and communicating them. It is as much an experience of *finding* out as it is of *letting* out what we feel. The very process of putting words to our feelings is an invitation to our experience to step out of the inner private world into the shared world of others, to emerge out of inchoate form into a form that can be known and talked about. This form, which is language, implies a commonality of meaning and the potential for validation in a community of others who can bear witness to what we are describing. It projects a sympathetic listener, whether one or many, whether inside or out, who receives our message just as, in this very moment, I project a sympathetic listener who is reading and comprehending what I now write. The prospect of being witnessed is what makes writing a healing art.

We can write for ourselves as in journal writing or in the writing of letters that we never plan to send. In both cases, the key is to let the feelings flow with a minimum of censorship or editing. The emphasis is on the process, not the product. I think of Gully Jimson, the prototypal artist in *The Horse's Mouth*, [52] who puts the finishing touch on the masterpiece of his life just as the wrecking ball swings to demolish the wall he has just painted it on.

You can think of your writing like that wall mural or like the tape in *Mission Impossible* that is about to self-destruct. It is the act of expressing your feelings that matters, not the form they take. I remind people that they are not writing for English 110 and there are no grades for grammar or spelling or how eloquently they rage or hate. The articulation of feelings carries the message that our feelings are intrinsically important and need to be acknowledged, like ourselves, not because they are good or bad but just because they exist.

As a final possibility, you may simply start writing and end up, as I did, writing *a book*.

5. Artistic expression

For those who are not inclined toward writing, there are many other forms of artistic expression that can accomplish the same goal. We can release angry feelings by singing them, dancing them, drawing them, painting them, or sculpting them out. We can make a mask or weave a tapestry. We can blast on a tuba or beat on a drum. In any of these varied modes of expression, the important thing to remember is to use fantasy to focus on the person or persons we are angry at. It is peace of mind we are creating, not masterpieces. The

52 Cary, Joyce: *The Horse's Mouth*, M. Joseph, London, 1944.

point is the expression, not the art.

As well as fantasy, *talking about* our angry feelings is the other main option that is available and is, undoubtedly, the choice most frequently employed. Most of us need to have somebody to complain to.

Nevertheless, though we may talk about our anger quite a bit, we are not necessarily successful at relieving or eradicating it. That will depend, in part, on how we are received. If we are required to justify or defend ourselves, if we are led to feel discounted or dismissed, we will continue to carry the anger or even expand on it. We will be most inclined in this instance to turn the anger, or at least some of it, against ourselves.

If, however, we find a caring acceptance of, though not necessarily agreement with, our angry feelings and an atmosphere of validation and respect, we will be more inclined to feel accepting of ourselves and to come away less angry or even, for the moment, anger-free. The experience of being *heard* makes a decisive difference to how talking about our anger feels.

The experience of being heard is contingent, we must add, not only on the response of the listener but also, at the same time, on the speaker's own pattern of response. If we project on whomever we meet in the present the unsympathetic witnesses of the past we will, not surprisingly, continue to feel angry and unheard. According to an anonymous quote left me by my mate:

"Spiritual development is...
  coming to terms with reality
  while not being bound byone's past."

By this definition, talking about our feelings should, ideally, be a facet of spiritual development. Certainly, therapy should exemplify this kind of healing talk.

We can talk to a therapist or we can talk to a friend. Sometimes the one can play the role of the other. Where they may diverge is that a therapist should, in principle, recognize those places where the false self needs to be confronted and where the shadow lurks and needs to come to light. While a friend may balk at pointing out our personal limits, a competent therapist will exhort us to face them and step beyond. The facing, owning, listening to, and celebrating of our angry and hateful feelings constitutes a crucial step in the process of becoming whole.

In whatever method we use, as we reclaim our anger and hatred, we will feel a resurgence of energy and power - not of power *over* others but of power *in* oneself, the boldness, the stalwartness, and the daring to say "Yes" to *all* of who we are.

*   *   *

In the next section, we will take up battle with the shadow on the other side of the teeter-totter, the side of defiance, our apparent strength.

Part Five

More Wrestling with the Shadow

Round Two: Neediness

He who gazes at stars
        is at the mercy of the puddles on the road.

Once we have made our peace, to some degree, with anger and hatred, the teeter-totter shifts and we come face to face with the other side. We feel separate and we know how to fight for ourselves. We have force on our side. Perhaps, as our mood is lifted higher, we might even taste the heady exhilaration of being dauntless and invincible. We drum our breasts, Tarzan-style. We are strong! We stand alone! We feel free!

Defiance gives us a sense of power. It will seem infinitely preferable to the submissiveness, the bowing and scraping of compliance. Words like "whining," "cringing," "maudlin," "pathetic," "dependent," "weak," and "cowardly" come to mind and will be greeted with revulsion. The images they conjure up are the epitome of what the defiant fears. It is the specter of our weakness, helplessness, and neediness that we turn from in horror, the shadow that defiance disavows.

We are reminded of the pitiable creature, Gollum, in Tolkien's *Lord of the Rings*, a character who whined and pleaded, groveled and hissed, and felt immeasurably sorry for himself.

He would cringe and flinch, if they stepped near him or made any sudden movement—but he was friendly, and pitifully anxious to please. He would cackle with laughter and caper, if any jest was made, or even if Frodo spoke kindly to him, and weep if Frodo rebuked him.[53]

Neediness exudes out of Gollum like a foul odor. He is a caricature of what we most fear. We see in him our own craving for approval and we are repulsed by it. We see our own pathetic victim role.

Yet Tolkien gives a hint of a link between strength and weakness, an insight we will return to later, when he says:

"For a moment it appeared to Sam that his master had grown and Gollum had shrunk: a tall, stern shadow, a mighty lord who hid his brightness in grey cloud, and at his feet a

53 Tolkien, J.R.R.: *Lord of the Rings, Part Two: The Two Towers*, Ballantine Books, New York, 1965, page 286.

whining dog. Yet the two were in some way akin and not alien: they could reach one another's minds." [54]

For most of us, the prospect of being like Gollum, a whipped cur reduced to helplessness, is a truly appalling one.

This utter helplessness is, perhaps, a too-poignant reminder of our own beginnings. Neediness is our natural condition. We are born into it. As infants, we start out this way. It is our lot in life to be born dependent and there are no exceptions, no infant wonders who can walk, talk or feed themselves from birth. That is just the way it is. Human beings, in comparison to all other species, remain dependent on caregivers for a remarkably long time.

Yet, for many of us, our neediness is unacceptable. We rail at it and feel ashamed of it; we hide it and deride it; we react to it with panic and despair. I often remind clients who are appalled at their own unprotesting tolerance of abuse in their childhoods: "What choice did you have? What three-year-old goes out to make a living? What five-year-old rents her own apartment? What seven-year-old can make it without his family there?" Sometimes we need a strong reminder of the inescapable reality of being a child.

Every one of us had times in our childhood when our needs were not met. It is virtually impossible for any parent, no matter how caring and dedicated, to anticipate and respond perfectly to all the needs of a child. The doorbell rings; we're on the phone; we don't feel well; we want time alone. There are so many demands both within and outside the family to respond to. The child, however central, is only one of them.

And even when we are focused on the child, we don't always respond in the best possible way. We miss the cues or misread them. There is interference from our own needs and projections. We don't feel loving at all times. Being a parent is a difficult job even when we are genuinely trying to do our best. Inevitably, we falter; we bungle; we mess it up. Sometimes we may also require a strong reminder of the

54 Ibid., page 285.

reality of being a parent.

Disappointment at the hands of our parents is thus inevitable. Nonetheless, it is inordinately hard to bear. We are so little, so helpless, so trapped in our dependency. Our needs are pressing, intense, and inescapable, yet we have so few resources to provide for ourselves.

As children, when our needs are not met, we experience frustration. We cry out to communicate our need. When our crying goes unheeded, our frustration increases and builds to an unadulterated rage. There is panic, fury, and desperation in that cry. As adults, we have all witnessed the twisted red-faced grimace of an infant screaming out its rage.

If the fever pitch continues unattended, eventually the exhausted infant will give up. The screaming trails off to a whimper. Then it stops. The child may go to sleep and bury the need altogether. Or it may rest and gather strength to wail anew. In some cases, though awake, the child goes listless. Its body sags, its eyes are blank. The rage is sucked inside and covered over. Even a tiny infant can show signs of being depressed.

While, inevitably, all of us experience some level of frustration in our childhood, there are definitely major differences of degree. The more frequently we are distressed and frustrated as children without any comfort or relief, the more this rage will become a defining characteristic of the personality. Goldberg refers to it as "narcissistic hate." [55]

This rage makes it difficult for us to trust others. We set up our own impenetrable barricade. We attempt through the creation of a defensive structure to ward off the experience of such profound and painful helplessness. Our personality is constructed around this central tenet: never to be needy again.

The paradox of this life stance is that while we attempt to avoid neediness, we are consumed by it. While we fabricate a bold exterior, we are inwardly driven by fear. What we cannot

---

55 *The Dark Side of Love*, page 73.

deal with acts upon us like a compulsion. We are, in a turn of phrase from a popular song, "caught in a masquerade."

In her book, *Obsessive Love,* Susan Forward examines the destructive effects of extreme frustration of our infantile needs. By way of illustration, she offers a striking vignette which, when I read it, lodged itself in my mind like a harpoon.

She is describing the conflict between the deep satisfaction of being connected with mother and the desire to separate and become an autonomous self. Noting that this conflict is turbulent for virtually all of us, even if we had parents who were generally responsive to our needs, she points out how much more torturous it will be for those of us who grew up in unhealthy families.

> If the separation process can be so easily disturbed in healthy families, imagine what happens if our parents frighten us, hurt us, abuse us, or neglect us on a regular basis. Such parents sabotage our separation by damaging the self-confidence, and confidence in others, that we need to continue on the path to independence. If we grow up in an unhealthy family, in an atmosphere where our needs for respect, love, approval, and protection are generally ignored or trampled, the disconnection process is more than interrupted, it is almost certainly derailed.[56]

Though we may, on the surface, appear to be increasingly independent, what we feel inside is a desperate desire to reconnect with that original, now-unattainable feeling of oneness and connection. This desire is more than just a yearning; it is, she says, an overwhelming compulsion. Then she continues:

> To get a better understanding of this compulsion, imagine a little child who leaves her happy cottage in the woods to see the world. Somewhere along the path, she comes upon a creature she's never seen before. Frightened,

---

56 Forward, Susan, *Obsessive Love* , Bantam Books, Toronto, June 1992, page 199.

she runs back home. The child from a healthy family finds comfort and reassurance when she gets there. Her parents investigate, determine that the creature is harmless, and encourage her to venture out the next day to try again.

But the child from an unhealthy family finds herself locked out. She pounds frantically on her front door, begging for help as she imagines the monster approaching behind her. She sees a light beneath the door, a ray of hope encouraging her to pound harder, but no one comes to save her. The harder she pounds, the more desperate she becomes to get in. [57]

Some of us may get stuck out there, pounding on a locked door, interminably.

Let us pause a moment to take in the impact of this picture. In this simple snapshot, I find a profoundly moving portrait of childhood suffering, almost, one might say, an archetype of primal pain. It contains within it all the elements of a traumatic experience that could be reenacted again and again: the terror, the aloneness, the abandonment, the disappointment, the confusion, the rage, the feeling of being betrayed, the frustration, the desperation, the torment, the grief, the despair, and the pain. In its simplicity is its power. This snapshot could be subtitled: "The Breaking of Trust."

It is no wonder that we are tempted to bury, deny or arm ourselves against this primal pain. It has a deep resonance in the psyche deriving from our earliest experiences of neediness and vulnerability.

If our neediness was habitually ignored, ridiculed, or punished, we will experience it as immeasurably painful. We will be anxious to turn the other way, endeavoring to put it behind us, acting as if it were not there. When we assume the defiant posture, it is as if we turn away from that ray of hope out of a conviction that the door will never open. Our hope is buried under bitterness or feigned unconcern. The locked-out child may stomp off in a huff and refuse to knock again.

57 Ibid., page 200.

Or she may start playing raucously by the door, making no further effort to get in, but covertly trying with laughter and loud noise to keep the unnamed creatures at bay.

We may act as if we are fun-loving and carefree, but we are lonely. We may look fiercely independent, but we are not. Our trust is in tatters. We are in shock. We carry the imprint of this traumatic experience in our psyches. Inwardly, we are unable to leave the scene.

Some familiar, not altogether endearing, qualities of defiant people are:

(1) We need to be right. We have difficulty admitting that we are wrong or that we make mistakes. We have unreasonably high expectations of ourselves.

(2) If there is a problem or difficulty, we tend to locate it in others, rather than in ourselves. We see other people's vulnerability and deny our own. We are inclined to be blamers.

(3) We have unreasonably high expectations of others. We are very demanding in relationships.

(4) We are generous in giving criticism but have difficulty accepting criticism of ourselves. We argue or get easily offended.

(5) We are controlling, though we likely don't perceive ourselves as such. We are known to rage or sulk if we don't get our way.

(6) We hide our vulnerability behind a smoke screen of anger. We may be intimidating to others.

(7) Though we feign indifference, we are actually very

deeply attached to others and may have inordinate difficulty with separation.

(8) We tend to be jealous and possessive. We perceive other people and interests in our loved ones' lives as a potential threat.

(9) We have difficulty with aloneness. We either fear and avidly avoid it or we become "loners" and cultivate it to an extreme.

(10) We are suspicious and quick to perceive rejection, abandonment and betrayal in other's people's actions.

The purpose of this characterization is not attack or criticism but understanding. If you are a defiant, or are in close relationship with one, it is crucial to recognize that underlying all these attitudes is a TRUST ISSUE. Some event, or pattern of events, taught us to approach relationships with fear and dread. There is a *reason* why we are this way. I find it helpful to visualize behind the mask of defiance a terrified child pounding on a door that would not open. And perhaps that terrifying creature we imagine as a monster in the woods behind us is our own neediness.

* * *

*We were the Campbell soup generation. Newly purchased television sets displayed scenes of ruddy-cheeked children rescued from the cold by a perfect smiling mother and big bowls of steaming hot soup. One just **knew** there was love in every bowl.*

My favorite was cream of mushroom soup. What more coveted prize than those juicy bits of mushroom nestled in the thick white cream! In eager anticipation, I would spoon them up, lick them off one by one, and line them neatly around the edge of the bowl saving them for last.

On evening, just as my soup was almost finished and I was about to claim my prize, my father ordered my bowl removed. As I watched the departing bowl with tear-filled eyes, he barked out: "Let this be a lesson to you! If you want something in life, grab it! If you wait, it will be gone!"

I cried and my mother brought the bowl back. Did I ever learn the lesson? I might have been spared many hours of mooning over lost mushrooms if my father had had his way.

My Dad was a great believer in object lessons. My sister and brother were avid followers of a particular comic strip that appeared in the Saturday newspaper. They rushed to the doorstep the minute it was delivered to devour the latest developments in the story. One weekend, my father ordered the paper to be placed on top of the china cabinet in the dining room where it could be seen but not opened until the following Wednesday night. They had to wait five long days each week from then on. The lesson here was patience. By some obscure reasoning known only to him, it made sense for one to grab mushrooms but wait for comic strips. My father was a man who could tolerate inconsistency without a flinch.

Many years later, my Dad gave my husband a self-winding watch, demonstrating with a flourish how he was to roll his wrist so that it would continue to work. Within a day or so, the watch stopped. No wrist-rolling seemed to help until my husband discovered a tiny knob that rewound the watch.

When they met again, my father inquired about the watch and how it was working.

"It works great, Dad," my husband said, "but it's not self-winding," and he explained what had happened with the watch.

Without a moment's hesitation, my father shot back indignantly: "That watch was self-winding when I gave it to you!"

At his deathbed, moments after he had breathed his last, I took my father's strength as my inheritance. It was this strength that saw my through the grueling challenges I put to myself, the times of crisis I endured alone. That strength was there when I decided to quit my job and travel to California, taking my very first trip on my own, despite a red neon sign blinking "Eat" at the window and sordid creatures, both animal and human, scuttling about.

It was there too, when I decided to move to Vancouver just weeks before my only friend in that city packed up and left on an around-the-world tour. It was there a month later when I lay in a hospital bed, not permitted to eat or drink, listening to the sounds of babies crying in the nursery next door and wondering if the one inside of me would live or die. For eleven hours I waited, by myself, with parched throat and aching heart to find out that, after years of trying to get pregnant and succeeding at last, I had had a miscarriage.

The strength I drew from my father was a toughness, a grim determination, a tightness in the jaw. It was a tenacity that kept me going against all odds. It was an insistence on "principle", on integrity, and on what was **right**. It was a single mindedness that brooked no weakness and no excuse.

Finally I came to realize that this was false strength, the puffed –up strength of the defiant position, the posture of bravado that covered a deep fear of vulnerability. It confused softness with weakness. It saw being wrong as an admission of failure, and giving **in** as giving **up**.

I wonder if my father had the same realization. When cancer racked his body and the pain forced him to tears, possibly for the first time in his life, he saw that we moved closer; we did not run away. After that, he developed a new gesture which took the place of the clenched fist and jaw. It was a gesture of surrender. I call it "the Albert Aarons shrug."

I learned that by experiencing the weakness that had been forced into the shadow, a new strength could emerge, a quality of presence that supports the true self rather than hiding it behind a mask of defiance.

I think my Dad glimpsed that presence before he died. He sat close to me just once, on the living room couch, in front of everyone in the family, holding my hand.

* * *

Because of the pain associated with our neediness, we turn away from it. It becomes repugnant to us. We do not care to be reminded of this disowned shadow part, whether these reminders are in ourselves or in others. I see flashes of my mate with one hand on his hip and his finger wagging as he shouted: "Face it! To live a complete and fulfilling life, you *need* me!" And there was I stomping off with my head proudly flung back, in a gesture of utter disdain. I would not admit to neediness then. But it appears he was right after all.[58]

Such reminders are, unfortunately, virtually impossible to avoid. Because of the pervasiveness of victimization, we are constantly tripping over instances of neediness, helplessness, and vulnerability both in us and around us. Because of the pervasiveness of emotional abuse, we see neediness shamed and not responded to. We see helplessness exploited and trampled on. We see vulnerability crushed with harshness and severity. How can we forget when the victim/abuser dance is all around?

When a child witnesses a victim/abuser interaction or is in the victim-abuser dance themselves, a pattern is set in motion for reenactment. We have seen how victimization sets up a cycle of continuing abuse.

As we found in Part Two, the victim, acting out of beliefs intrinsic to the role of victim, tends to unconsciously perpetuate the experience of abuse. The power to abort this destructive pattern is projected on the abuser and is not seen as existing in the self. Therefore, we perceive it as a necessity, for the sake of survival, to seek approval from the other. Compliance is the form which this need for approval takes.

At the same time, the victim identifies with the abuser and grants validity to the abuser perspective. From the one-down position of the victim, particularly when the victim is

---

58 Andrew Feldmar rightly points out that neediness in general does not entail neediness for any specific person. He argues that specific statements of need such as "I need you" or "you need me" constitute emotional blackmail. The correct formulation, according to Feldmar, would be in terms not of "need" but of "desire".

a child, it must seem that right stands on the side of might, at least the vast percentage of the time.

Moreover, might is exceptionally appealing. The child, perpetually confronted with examples of his or her own severely limited strengths and capabilities, is attracted to the power of the abuser position. S/he wants to enjoy that power too. Think of how a child will exuberantly scold the dog, wallop the cat, or whack a stuffed doll (or an unfortunate younger sibling) with unabashed glee. Before we learn to camouflage our blatant enjoyment, it seems undeniable that being abusive is *fun*.

By nature, we take pleasure in the sheer exercise of power. We take pleasure in overpowering those who prove to be weaker and more helpless than ourselves. Though we are loath to admit it, triumph over others brings with it exhilaration and its own form of adrenaline rush.

Some of the pleasure of the triumph is in retaliation. Somewhere, some time, we have been on the down side of the power play. We seek revenge for those times we have endured the humiliation of having our noses rubbed in our helplessness. We want to give back what we have received, "an eye for an eye" as the Bible says. Thus, abuse of power is contagious. We get infected, then we pass it on. Like an infection, the abuse spreads rapidly. Pretty soon it reaches epidemic proportions. What we pass on, keeps coming back to us. We get caught up in the cycle of abuse.

The underlying factor that propels this cycle is the collapse of basic trust. The environment that should have been a supportive holding for us turns out to be hurtful. What should have held us lets us down. What should have contained us springs leaks. The body contracts in nervous tension and stiffens in an effort to carry on. We begin to lose that natural confidence in our existence, that sense of ease in being alive. Instead of a light, relaxed resting in living process, we become suspicious and poised to fight. We assume defensive postures in an attempt to feel safe and secure in a world we no longer trust. We become consumed with strategies of protection. In place of cooperation, we seek control.

The effect of this breakdown of trust, though it may have originated in the distant past, is felt and experienced *in the now*. It is in our characteristic patterns of holding stress and tension in our bodies. It is in the beliefs we carry about ourselves in relation to the universe and other beings. It shows itself in the feverish ongoing efforts we make to control the future: to plan ahead, to be prepared, to have enough, to ward off disaster, to get a handle, to have it "made." It is evident in the constant efforts we make to control other people: to please, to impress, to resist, to persuade, to dominate, to manipulate. It is in our hyper-vigilance, our on-guardness, our expectation of being hurt, now, because we were hurt before, back then. The past is carried with us. In this sense, it is here now, waiting to be reckoned with.

* * *

According to the family story, when I was born and my mother brought me home from the hospital, my brother came running. What a profound disappointment he had when he saw me. He was hoping for a **puppy***!*

I never outgrew this feeling of being a disappointment to him. I took it on. It was my fault; it was something wrong with me. Since he was wonderful, the disappointment, the one who didn't measure up, had to be me.

In order to maintain this illusion, I had to deny a good part of reality. If he knew more, then I was stupid. If he was stronger, then I was weak. I had to close my eyes to what he did to me or, even worse, convince myself that I deserved whatever I received.

How desperately I longed to be his friend! It was as if, through blind devotion, I was trying to be the eager and unfailing ally that a puppy might have been. I put my utmost faith in him despite repeated demonstrations that it was misplaced. I still prickle with shame when I recall the times he exposed my deepest, darkest secrets in front on my friends. When I surreptitiously signaled him to silence, he pointed this out, jeeringly, to everyone. There was no safe alliance with him.

From my brother I learned powerlessness and how to repress rage. Being five years older, he always had the edge. He was five years bigger, five years stronger, more experienced, and smarter than I. When it was "cool" to be one-up, naturally my brother wanted to be cool. He became a master of the sarcastic put-down.

What more perfect practice target than his fawning little sister. For years I endured a relentless stream of put-downs that mocked me in the guise of humor and drew countless laughs at my expense. Often his jibes were directed at my appearance, particularly my less than amply developed breasts which he frequently compared to an ironing board. When I was entering puberty, he told me that no man would ever want me for my body. I believed him absolutely. You may marvel at my gullibility but I had him on a pedestal. Through his eyes, I learned to hate my body. And I carried this hatred for years.

He explained, years later, that he had belittled my appearance for my own good so that I would not be vain and conceited like most of the girls in our neighborhood. "Jewish American Princesses" he called them, transporting a term from across the border. Nor was the message lost on me when I was dubbed "princess" in our family. It was not a term of endearment as in the notion of beautiful princesses awaiting magical princes in the fairy tales. I knew that was not for me. My princess title was combined with "spoiled" as in "spoiled brat" and "spoiled rotten." To me, it meant ruined, disgusting, annoying and bad.

By the time I was in high school, my brother had become quite obese but I denied this. He was "chubby," he insisted, while others snickered with amusement. Then he contracted typhoid fever and almost died because the doctors were unable to make a diagnosis for quite a long time. Immediately upon his recovery, he got married and moved out. It was as though I lost him twice. Increasingly, he hid behind his fat and I never felt connected with him again. Maybe nobody did.

But I was set up for a reenactment. My brother was my hero. I loved an image whose perfection seemed to confirm my deficiency. To my unending exasperation, my brother was always better than me, no matter how I tried. To redeem myself I had to fight him. Yet when I fought, I was inevitably defeated.

The truth is: it was not my fault. I could not have been on equal terms with him as a child. Though in retrospect it sounds incredible, what I failed to take into account was the power differential between us and the fact that he took unfair advantage of me. When I was very little, he used to exchange my dimes for nickels because, he argued, they were bigger. The glaring truth that I refused to see was that he was bigger too, by five years, and though not necessarily worth more, he did know better. To see myself as a victim, I had to see him as an abuser. My idol was a **bully**.

It is true that he had been a victim too. My father bullied him mercilessly, calling him a sissy and a little girl if he ever cried or showed any softness or emotion. As he was taught to despise vulnerability in himself so, of course, he would despise it when he saw it in me. He was trained systematically to be hard and cold in the name of being a man. And he learned so well at least in part, because he practiced on me.

Finally it was my turn to get the message. His one-up-manship was not strength, it was weakness. This was not love; it was abuse. Bullying someone who has less power is not proof of the victim's inferiority but of the abuser's need to dominate. It is sadistic like "a boot stomping on a human face forever" [59] and inexorable like the cycle of abuse. What my father acted out on my brother, my brother acted out on me. Is it any wonder that the cycle repeated in my marriage?

Only when we can see the murderer in the saint and the saint in the murderer will we have the possibility of seeing human beings in their wholeness and of letting go of the need to coerce and dominate.

59 Orwell, George: *Nineteen Eighty-Four*, page 280.

*   *   *

Knowing how our trust got broken is a first step toward becoming free of the reenactment cycle. Knowing where we got "derailed" is a beginning of being able to step away from the doorway and move on.

The more information we have about the ways in which our family of origin responded, for better and for worse, to our neediness as children, the more possibility we will have of disengaging from the tragic reenactment of our early disappointments and hurts. The process of acquiring this knowledge about our history and its impact on us is called *demystification*. It is a breaking free of the myths and illusions we carry about our families.

Much of therapy is demystification. Therapy is, or should be, an alliance to free ourselves of the limiting beliefs, feelings, and patterns of relating that come primarily out of our early childhood and have been unconsciously reenacted ever since.

Undoubtedly, it is the present-day impediment we are experiencing in our lives that first brings us into therapy and becomes its initial focus. But the root is almost always in the past.

I frequently remark at the beginning of therapy, that "I am not an archaeologist who likes to dig up and study old bones for their own sake." These beliefs, feelings and modes of relating are not a matter of ancient history. They are present; they are active today. But usually they are unconscious or, we may prefer to say, out of our awareness. Therefore, the art of therapy is to get access to this material, to find ways to bring it into our awareness, "to make the unconscious conscious" as Freud used to say.

This task is particularly difficult for defiant people in view of the fact that our solution to the painfulness of early disappointment and frustration is to be oppositional. We turn *against.* This turning is not only against those who might have, even should have, filled our needs, but is also directed against the needs themselves. We simply don't want to have them. We may be stubborn, feisty, diffident, aloof or cavalier, depending on stylistics but, in one way or another, we resist being dependent. Our favorite saying is: *I Can Do It Myself!*

For this reason, defiants may resist therapy. We may not be able to admit that we need help. We are not inclined to ask for support or to acknowledge that we need it unless circumstances, or our partners, force us. We usually come to therapy, if at all, through some life crisis - a separation, a death, a disease, a failure - and, sometimes, by being therapists ourselves.

* * *

I thought I had learned the lesson of defiance when my mate left and the over-functioning professional woman/single mother that I was by day transformed into a weeping, wailing, thumb-sucking child by night. The hidden message of defiance was writ large, I thought, in my deep inconsolable longing. Three years and my heart still ached every time I thought of him. What greater proof could there be of my neediness?

It took a debilitating disease to force the lesson deeper, the crumbling of my over-functioning persona to drive the lesson home. Neediness is more profound, more elemental, paralyzing and inescapable than I had let myself acknowledge. This knowledge, hammered home through pain and illness, would crush whatever husk remained of my defiant shell.

When I first heard the diagnosis of Chronic Fatigue Syndrome and Fibromyalgia, the doctor's face was tired, grey and worn. I remember feeling sorry for him. Certain of his phrases fluttered in my mind like bits of old newspaper blown by the wind on a late fall day. "No treatment," "Nothing I can recommend," "We don't really understand," "Just rest," "No cure." Fragments of my life fluttered to the ground like out-of-date, crumpled newspapers, never to be read again. What an "incurable" disease meant to me was that, like life, there was no escape from it - except through death. I got much sicker after that.

Within a couple of months, I began to feel better and (which was first?) I began to wonder if it was the diagnosis or the disease that had made me ill. So I consulted another doctor.

This man was a good deal more positive than the first, smiling and peppering his delivery with messages like "Can Improve," "Progress is Possible," "Learn to Live With," "Can Heal," but the diagnosis was the same. I scored eleven out of thirteen on the Chronic Fatigue symptoms and fourteen out of eighteen on the Fibromyalgia trigger points. For an achievement-oriented, grade-seeking academic type like me, this was one A rating I could have done without! However, I was feeling better then. I recall telling the doctor that I was already well on the path to recovery and musing to myself on whether I should write about it in my book.

A month later, I was sick again. My therapy practice had been declining at a remarkable rate, my book was at a standstill, my dog had died, my spiritual training group was riddled with conflict, and my kids had decided they hated each other. (Had they read Part Four? I wondered.)

I was lying in bed fully dressed, huddled under the covers, with the heated mattress pad turned up to high and my limbs ice cold. It was a writing day, but I was not able to write. My body was stuck in bed and my writing was stuck in Part Five.

I remembered a story told by Ram Dass about a friend of his who, after struggling for years to overcome a drug problem, had finally succeeded in getting accepted into law school. At the same time, he was diagnosed with terminal cancer. "Promoted to the Advanced class!" Ram Dass had said. I knew I would never advance to the next class until I faced the question: What was my disease here to teach me?

I posted a sentry at the observation station of my mind on one of my Bad Days ("everyone has them," everyone says) and took notes.

9 o'clock:

I have a whole day to write! I've weathered squawks from the kids about having to go to the Y and mutterings from my Superego about my failing bank account to get this day to write. I promise I will do nothing else ... as soon as I get these few dishes out of the way ... and these few phone calls made ... and the laundry on...

10 o'clock:

I still have five hours left. (I settle down on the bed with my warm mug and my notepaper.) Now what was it I was going to write about? God, my fingers hurt when I hold the pen. And what are these pains shooting up my arms? my legs? my back? I'll just lie down. Now what was I going to write about today? Oh, yeah, the pain. What is the meaning of this pain? What is this illness teaching me? (I close my eyes to think.)

12 o'clock:

Oh God, I fell asleep! I worked so hard to get this time to write and then I blow it all away! What an idiot I am! Never mind, I still have almost three hours left. I probably needed the sleep to think straight anyway. Thinking is hard these days. Words slip away. I feel their presence but they slide away from me, escaping into the fog, snickering at my inability to catch them. I used to be so bright, so razor sharp! Analytic wonder of the Philosophy department. Scholarship lady. What's happened to my mind? It's this damn disease. I go into a daze. Can't trust my body; can't trust my mind. What's left? If I can't trust my body and I can't trust my mind, then I can't trust me! It was bad enough to discover I couldn't trust other people, but I thought for sure I could count on me. Here I am, I'm fifty, and I'm like a ninety year old lady hobbling around. I can almost see her at my side, the old "fogy"!

1 o'clock:

I hobble downstairs to get a chocolate chip muffin out of the freezer and hobble back upstairs, holding on tightly to the railing. I cut the muffin into four quarters and put three away. As I eat one quarter, a voice inside reminds me, "you were going to lose weight!" Slowly, one after the other, I eat the other three quarters.

I refill my water and sit back down, steering my thoughts back to the notepaper. "Chronic Fatigue and lack of basic trust" is written at the top of the page.) Chronic fatigue is like God making His point with a two-by-four. What is His point anyway? I have a list of grievances cycling through my head. I want to present my list to God and to the whole universe like a devastatingly powerful defense lawyer mounting an irrefutable case. I want the members of the jury to gasp with indignation at what has befallen me and the courtroom spectators to clamor loudly on my behalf. I want the gavel to fall with a resounding crack, granting me justice and compensation. My health back and my mate. What a joke! I feel ashamed of my foolishness. I'm crying. Could I be crying? It's not me that's crying. It's that old "fogy" again.

2 o'clock:

Soon, very soon, I'll have to squeeze my feet into my shoes and go pick up the children. The phone is ringing for the umpteenth time. (I hear the duck phone quacking at me and I ignore it until, gratefully, I hear the answering machine pick up the call.) No doubt, someone wants me to go somewhere or do something I don't want to do. Anyway I don't have the time or the strength or the energy. I feel exhausted. What have I accomplished today? Nothing! I'm still stuck in Part Five and I haven't even started that part about pain and lack of trust. I gotta get the bed made before the kids come home. Do it quick and get it over with so it doesn't hurt too long. Could it be significant that it's so hard for me to bend? Is that old lady at my side a feisty old coot who waves curses at God with her cane? But I've already worked on anger and hatred. That was Part Four. I need a piece on neediness now.

2:45:

(I struggle to my feet.) A piece on neediness? What do you think this is?!

* * *

Most often it is some life crisis such as a disease, a personal failure that we take to heart, or the loss of a loved one that plunges us into the shadow side of our defiance and mires us in our neediness. The intensity of our reaction is a consequence of its being a mirroring of our early past.

In these moments of crisis, we have an opportunity to access the repressed pain of the past and, by understanding and demystifying it, to begin to release its hold. We do not have to wait for a life crisis, however. We can begin this process at any time. Perhaps reading this chapter will be the stimulus that convinces you that now is the very best time. In the light of this possibility, I will offer a few pointers to get you started on your way.

There are a number of demystification techniques or access routes, we might call them, to get to the past in the present. I will highlight a few of them here. These are the "stuff" of therapy, the distinctive offerings of each individual therapeutic school. You can follow one or a combination of approaches, and I do not intend to advocate one particular approach or style of therapy here.

The one recommendation I do make is that it is best to do this work with a therapist you trust, rather than strictly on your own. The reason is that, as we move beyond our defensive structures to expose the neediness that lies below, we will surface the primal terror, helplessness, and pain we felt as children. Having a strong, secure holding environment is crucial if we are to face our utter defenselessness without fleeing into the escape routes we sought before. In the therapeutic alliance, we experience the holding, the bonding that we missed in our early lives. Ironically, it is this very experience of trust and holding that may enable us to become conscious of our inner pain about that which we missed before.

It has been said that our entire history is recorded in our body if we could but read it. Interestingly, the same has been said of the unconscious mind which is thought to contain in its memory banks all the experiences we have ever had since the beginning of our existence (some would say birth, others conception, and still others go back even further). To gain access to this information, certain approaches go through the body and others go through the mind. We might say they are different keys to the same door.

Body work is based on the principle that the modes of defense we adopted to protect our vulnerability have become incorporated in us as chronic patterns of tension in the body. Sometimes referred to as the "body armor," these areas of tension are the entry point to our early experiences of trauma, both large and small. I will not go into detail about the theory justifying body work,[60] because the experience will speak for itself. Body work is perhaps the most direct way of tapping into the unconscious and reliving the past in the now.

Hypnotherapy is another effective vehicle for accessing the unconscious mind. By inquiring about a problem in the present, we can track it back to its earliest antecedents and trigger memories long buried in the past.

There are a variety of tracking methods used by hypnotherapists such as ideo-motor questioning,[61] structured

---

60 For more information about the theory of bodywork, see Reich, William: *The Function of the Orgasm*, Orgone Institute Press, New York, 1942 or the more recent writings of Alexander Lowen such as *Love and Orgasm*, Macmillan, New York, 1965, *The Betrayal of the Body*, Macmillan, New York, 1967, *The Language of the Body*, Macmillan, New York, 1971, Bioenergetics, Penguin Books, New York, 1975.
61 See the pioneer work of Cheek, David and LeCron Leslie: *Clinical Hypnotherapy*, Grune & Stratton, A Subsidiary of Harcourt Brace Jovanovich Publishers, New York, 1968.

fantasy, and a remarkably powerful technique called "the affect bridge." [62] In the latter, the feeling in the present, magnified and detached, becomes the spring-board for associational roots going deep into the past. For example, my feeling of longing, though currently focused on my mate, would take me into the pain of a long succession of childhood experiences of missing my mother. In using affect as a bridge, this method capitalizes on an awareness that many of us have, albeit dimly, that the link between present and past may be of a feeling nature, rather than a sensory one. For instance, my mate may not *look* much like my mother, but the way I react may be the same. Hypnotherapy puts its trust in unconscious process to surface these connections.

We can also ferret out connections in a more analytical way. We can look for "themes" - that is, patterns of acting and interacting that reappear in different time frames and in different situations throughout our lives much as if we were employing different scenery and characters to play out the same basic script. Noticing these repetitive patterns is what I refer to as *detective work*. It is with a feeling of adventure and intrigue that, in therapy, we don the proverbial Sherlock Holmes hat and look together for clues to the unsolved mysteries of a person's life.

Besides analysis, we can use the *processing* of immediate experience to uncover connections in the context of working with a therapist or in working on our own. Many books are available which show examples of how expert therapists from different schools do their processing with clients (for example, see Perls' *Gestalt Therapy Verbatim* [63] or the Mindells' *Riding the Horse Backwards* [64] for actual transcripts of workshops conducted at Esalen Institute.) Other books offer exercises to be followed on your own - for example, *Homecoming* by John

---

62 Watkins, John G., "The Affect Bridge: A Hypnoanalytic Technique" *The International Journal of Clinical and Experimental Hypnosis*, 1971 Vol. X1X No. 1, pages 21-27.
63 Perls, Frederick S: *Gestalt Therapy Verbatim*, Bantam Books, New York, 1969.
64 Mindell, Arnold and Amy: *Riding the Horse Backwards: Process Work in Theory and Practice*, Arkana published by the Penguin Group, London, 1992.

Bradshaw [65] or the extremely handy little book by Eugene Gendlin entitled *Focusing*.[66] To enrich the smorgasbord of offerings, I have my own simple model to add to the list. I call it "the split screen" approach.

What follows is, in essence, an interrogative orientation - that is, a way of questioning your experience so that it yields up more depth. It does not pose answers, only questions, that will direct your search.

The first question is:

(1) what am I feeling right now?

Like the affect bridge, split screen begins with a current feeling (or feelings) and places that awareness on center screen.

To delve more deeply into this feeling (I will speak in the singular because you can do the same with each feeling that presents), we can inquire into the context in which this feeling emerged.

(2) when did this feeling start?

E.g. *I did not have it before lunch. I definitely had it after lunch. What happened during lunch?*

Context is more than merely temporal. It is also situational and relational. So we need to ask:

(3) who was there? what did they do? what did they say? what was the situation? how was I feeling about it? how do I feel about this feeling?

E.g. *At lunch time, my co-worker sat with the boss at a different*

---

65 Bradshaw, John: *Homecoming: Reclaiming and Championing Your Inner Child*, Bantam Books, New York, 1992.
66 Gendlin, Eugene T.: *Focusing*, 2nd edition, Bantam Books, New York, 1981.

table. I felt excluded and wondered if they were talking about me. Are they saying bad things? Why do I care what they say about me anyway?

We can also explore the nature of the feeling by asking:

(4) what kind of feeling is this?

In the broadest terms, feelings can be categorized under headings of basic family types. The topography I use is:

JOY   SADNESS   ANGER   FEAR

also known as:
GLAD   SAD   MAD   SCARED

Although it can sometimes happen that a feeling occupies more than one category, it will generally prove most useful to determine to what basic family a particular feeling belongs.

E.g. Am I sad or angry about being excluded? Or am I primarily scared?

We can generate more specific detail about a feeling by exploring its intensity and nuance of meaning. It will be instructive to keep asking the question: Can I be even *more* specific?

E.g. Okay, I know my reaction is in the anger family. Am I piqued, slightly irritated, considerably vexed, raging inside, or ready to kill? Is this a sort of outraged feeling as in "how dare you...?" or more of a snit as in "Who cares about you anyway?" Is it the kind of snit I get into when my pride has been hurt? Do I feel shame? Am I angry because I feel exposed as someone they don't want to have lunch with?

To get clearer about the nature of a feeling, we can also explore its associations. We can ask:

(5) What images accompany this feeling? If I let myself, what might I fantasize doing or saying? If I had a magic wand, what would I wish to happen? And then where would that lead?

E.g. *I see myself kinda hunched over and dejected-looking. I wish I could just disappear. If I had a magic wand, I would make the boss invite me over to her table and send that other person packing! I want to be in her place. I guess it's envy I'm feeling.*

Images are not always visual. They can be kinesthetic or auditory. We may have bodily sensations that lead us to an awareness of what we are feeling.

E.g. *My stomach is clenching and so is my fist. Am I ever angry!*

Sometimes we hear words, phrases, or whole dialogues unfolding in our heads as we track what we feel. It is important to feel, look and listen all at the same time.

Should images not immediately spring to mind, the unconscious may offer us clues in other ingenious ways. If we turn to a blank page and just put down whatever arises spontaneously, in a relaxed kind of doodling, we may be surprised at the significance the words or images convey. Similarly, it is always revealing to listen in to the songs that are running through our minds.

E.g. *If I'm hearing "Nobody Knows the Trouble I've Seen," could it be that I am feeling sorry for myself?*

We might picture this line of questioning about the nature of each feeling as a "horizontal" exploration in contradistinction from one that is "vertical." In the latter case, we look at feelings as if they were layered one upon another and ask:

(6) What feeling is under that? Is there another one under that? And yet another?

E.g. *I'm angry at my boss for showing favoritism. I guess under the anger I'm hurt. Why doesn't she seem to like me? I'm afraid there is something wrong with me. I feel that a lot. Underneath my anger and fear, I realize I am not liking myself very much.*

Focusing on center screen, we can penetrate deeper and deeper layers of feeling that are present in the here and now.

To continue, we also need to inquire about the connections between the present and the past. I envisage this as filling in the left screen: the place of the past. We can ask:

(7) What does this feeling remind me of? Where and when have I felt this way before?

On the left screen, we are seeking the early sources and origins of our present experience. The springboard to the past is the moment-to-moment awareness of the present. Focus intently and let the data be your guide. If a visual image presents, see it clearly and then let it blur, allowing another image to emerge from behind the first. If it is an auditory image, listen closely and stay attuned to echoes and resonances from an earlier time. Similarly, if it is kinesthetic, attend closely to the way it feels. Allowing ourselves to feel our bodily sensations in minute and exquisite detail may lead us into the past if we are open and willing to be led.

We will also discover that one type of sensation may lead to a different type (visual to auditory, auditory to kinesthetic, etc.), crossing channels as it were. (In fact, Mindell's[67] methodology uses just this channel-crossing capacity to stretch us into new awarenesses.) We can ask of a feeling, for example: What are the words that go with this? When did I hear them before? What is the scene I am picturing? Who is with me there? What am I aware of in my body? How old do I feel?

E.g. *I see the two of them sitting with their heads together talking at the table. As the vision blurs, I see my mother and sister with their heads together having a similar conversation in the past. I am about seven. I am feeling left out and I hate my sister at this moment. The truth is, I am envious of her. I want to be closer to my Mom, but I never told her. I feel this tightness in my jaw as I clamp down and say nothing. I am scared I might be rejected. I thought she liked my sister more.*

Processing could be endless, so how do we know when to stop? I suggest what I call "the R or R rule" which is: go for Relief or Recognition. A point comes when we notice that the pattern that was previously blurry becomes clear, the voice that was distant is heard, the muscles that were tense relax. There is a subtle release, a kind of letting go, or feeling of completion. Some people call it "a click" or "a mini-Aha!" Sometimes completion brings a wave of release and relief. However, relief does not always occur. At other times when we recognize the connections, we feel the pain, rage or terror that was formerly suppressed. In these cases, we may not feel relieved but we will feel clear. Thus I suggest the Relief *or* Recognition rule.

Our final task is to go to right screen: directions for the future. Here we need to ask:

(8) What would help me feel better? What is it that needs

---

67 Mindell, Arnold: *Working With the Dreaming Body*, Arkana published by the Penguin Group, London, 1989, see Chapter four.

to change? Which attitudes of mine are outmoded? Which beliefs are out of date? What can I do in the present? What might I do in the future? How could I prevent this from recurring? What do I need to learn? What is my role in this problem? What is the message here?

E.g. I need to address my self-esteem issue. Obviously, if I don't feel good about myself, I can't expect other people to appreciate me. And I see now how I am mixing up my boss with my mother. My fear from the past is ruling me today. Maybe I could invite my boss out for lunch and get to know her better. The worst that could happen is that she would say no. I think I could handle that. I will ask.

Before we quit the field, it may be intriguing to pose one more question to see if it ensnares anything else. We might inquire:

(9) What, if anything, might I be denying here? What is it I am attached to and insisting upon? Is this my truth or my protection from truth? Is there a shadow side to what I believe is so?

E.g. I believed that my mother preferred my sister, but is this really so? Is this the true reason why I held back from my mother and refused to become close? Could it be that I was punishing her for giving her attention to someone else? I wanted all of it and I didn't want to share.

Ultimately, only we can be arbiters of truth for ourselves. As a client once remarked with startling aptness: Why do I always imagine there is someone with *more seniority?*

A Processing Model		
LEFT SCREEN	CENTER SCREEN	RIGHT SCREEN
The Past	The Present	The Future
What does this remind me of?	What am I feeling right now?	What would help me to feel better?
Where did I feel this way?	When did this feeling start?	What needs to change?
When did I feel this way before?	What was the situation in detail?	What can I do now?
What images accompanied this feeling?	What kind of feeling is this?	What can I do in the future?
What feeling is under that?	What feeling is under that?	What is my role in the problem?
	What might I be denying here?	What is the message here?

The demystification process will bring us closer and closer into connection with the truth of our own history. It may not be as we were told. It may be that those who told us did not know the truth themselves. More often than not, what we discover is that we were lied to, misled, or deceived, to a greater or lesser degree. The truth may not be pretty. Often adults want to protect their children from the truth. Just as often, they want to protect themselves. But whatever the intention, deception creates a rupture in our basic trust. It fractures the holding. It leaves our sense of reality shattered with no easy way to mend it. However painful and unpalatable, truth is the only healer. It gives us back our integrity, our sense of self.

Through the eye of innocence, with our trust intact, William Blake captures with poignancy our first vision of life:

"I have no name:
"I am but two days old."
 What shall I call thee?
"I happy am,
"Joy is my name."
 Sweet joy befall thee!

Pretty joy!
Sweet joy but two days old,
Sweet joy I call thee:
Thou dost smile,
I sing the while,
Sweet joy befall thee!

"Infant Joy" in *Songs of Innocence*[68]

Through the eye of experience, with the knowledge of suffering, Blake compels us to behold our changed vision of life:

My mother groan'd! My father wept.
Into the dangerous world I leapt:
Helpless, naked, piping loud:
Like a fiend hid in a cloud.

Struggling in my father's hands,
Striving against my swadling bands.
Bound and weary I thought best
To sulk upon my mother's breast.

"Infant Sorrow" in *Songs of Experience*[69]

*   *   *

---

68 "Songs of Innocence" in *William Blake*, Introduced and Edited by J. Bronowski, Penguin Books, Harmondsworth, Middlesex, England, 1958, page 37.
69 "Songs of Experience" in *William Blake*, page 54.

Inspired by Blake and caught up in the issue of basic trust and deception, I wrote my own song of innocence and experience. I call it:

A Wishing Song

(Can be sung or recited. You can join in the chorus on any of the wishing parts.)

> Star light, star bright,
> First star I see tonight.
> Wish I may, wish I might
> Have the wish I wish tonight.

Every night at bedtime I .... wished upon a star.

Every night they sat me on the railing in the hallway to look out the window and .... wish upon a star.

Every night in my pajamas, supported from falling, I sat above the staircase and .... wished upon a star.

Every night with my teeth brushed, I would gaze out the little window in the door to the porch to ....wish upon a star.

Every night I whispered to the light beyond the window the innermost dreams I........................... wished upon a star.

> Star light, star bright,
> First star I see tonight.
> Wish I may, wish I might
> Have the wish I wish tonight.

Every night, unfailingly, my star was always there.

> Every night the star was bright,
> Receiving in its glowing light
> Every wish a child could wish,
> Year after year.

Star light, star bright,
I always had a star at night.
Whatever the weather,
My star was always there.

Every night it shone for me, constant and immutable, as I gazed out the window, saying my prayer.

Star light, star bright,
First star I see tonight.
Wish I may, wish I might
Have the wish I wish tonight.

I must have been quite old when I found out. There was something *wrong* in this picture.

All those years, I had been wishing on .... *a street lamp.*

*   *   *

I could use the skills of conceptual analysis I had developed as a philosopher to ask:

Given that the flat roof beyond the window through which I wished was referred to as "a porch" by my family:

Was it a "porch" if it had no railing? Was it a "porch" if one got to it through a door? Was it a "porch" if nobody was allowed to go out on it? Was it a "porch" if it didn't function as a porch?

Mutatis mutandis, (philosopher-talk for: by the same argument,)

Given that the light beyond the window through which I wished was referred to as "a star" by my family:

Was it a "star" if it wasn't in the heavens? Was it a "star" if it glowed and was wished upon? Was it a "star" if only in a child's imagination? Was it a "star" if it functioned as a star?

This experience lends itself to analysis on a spiritual as well as linguistic dimension:

What is the spiritual significance of the "star" both as an

icon and as a transcendent object toward which the soul's yearning is addressed? When the star is exposed as a street lamp, is it the icon or the transcendent object that is thus unmasked? Is this not tantamount to a spiritual crisis? How is such a crisis to be healed?

From a spiritual perspective, is it clear that the star-gazer is in illusion or could it be that she saw a truth? Did the star turn into a street lamp or did the child turn away from the light? Is this a universe in which wishes are granted or even one in which wishes are heard? Is there, as Buber[70] says, a "Thou" out there to respond to my "I"? And "If I cry out," as the poem beseeches, "who among all heaven's angels will hear me?"

Or I could use the skills of psychological analysis I had developed as a therapist to ask:

How was this experience significant in the development of basic trust? How is it connected to the recurring theme of betrayal in this person's life?

What does it tell us about the role of truth in this family system? How do we evaluate the positive holding contained in this ritualized fantasy as against the trauma of shattered illusion when the truth comes out?

What bearing has it on the subject's extreme preoccupation with the distinction between fantasy and truth? How does it impact on her intimate relationships and her impoverished capacity for trust? Could we say this person went through life wishing on a star that turned out to be a street lamp? Could we say this was the story of her life?

*   *   *

Isn't it like wishing on a star to continue loving someone who will not even acknowledge you exist? Wouldn't it be like the star being exposed as a street lamp when the person you commit to marry and buy a house with walks out and never speaks to you again? Is it better to keep on wishing or close your heart to love?

My little niece once had a goldfish. She was only three or four

70 Buber, Martin: *I & Thou*, Charles Scribner's Sons, New York, 1958.

*years old at the time. She was surprised one day to see her mother
drop her goldfish into the toilet bowl. Softly my sister explained
to her that the goldfish was dead. Together they watched as the
goldfish swirled around in the flushing water and then disappeared
from sight. It was a sad moment for them both.*

*The next day my sister found her daughter in the bathroom
shaking fish food down the toilet bowl.*

*"What are you doing, dear?" my sister asked in puzzlement.
"You know that your fish is dead."*

*"I know that," my niece replied somberly, "but it still has to
eat."*

*Was I, in loving someone who was not responsive, feeding a
fish that was already dead?*

* * *

Here we stand face to face with the pain. Neediness,
broken trust, deception and disappointment - under the
defiant armor, our soft underbelly is revealed. Yet we have
also seen in ourselves the capacity to be the perpetrators, how
our pain leads us to hurt others as we have been hurt.

The work we have done on the shadow has brought us to
a place of new understanding. We have seen what happened
in our history as we shelved our anger and became compliant
or hid our neediness and became defiant. We have become
acquainted with our own disowned selves.

The self which emerges may be spindly from lack of
nourishment, embittered from long abuse, alienated from
lack of bonding, confused and anxious from being separated
from the truth. This self needs to be supported and fully
acknowledged. It is like a wayward child returning to its
home. As was implied in Tolkien's image at the beginning of
the chapter, true strength is in accepting our weakness; true
compassion is in realizing our hate.

The more we can be *for ourselves* the parents we wished we
had, the less defensive we will need to be. We will no longer

be perpetually at risk of a reenactment. The world will not seem like such a terrifying place. Because support comes from within rather than from outside us, we are not reactive all the time. We feel grounded. We feel held. We are on our way to being whole.

Being whole, means accepting ourselves for who we are even, paradoxically, if we are not yet wholly accepting. It means not judging ourselves for judging ourselves - or (even) not judging ourselves for judging ourselves for judging ourselves - if you follow where this leads. Somewhere the endless scramble has to stop. It's not easy to look ourselves straight in the eye, *without* illusions, and say wholeheartedly "I am okay." To be a sympathetic witness requires a special kind of courage, the courage to hold the truth.

*   *   *

All of a sudden and quite unexpectedly, it didn't seem like such a big deal. By "it" I mean all the abuses. So he did this and she did that to me. So they put me down. So they left me alone every time I was in need. So I was abandoned. So I was not welcome. So what?

The upshot is: I did manage in spite of my dysfunctional relationships and my dysfunctional family of origin. In spite of it all, here I am, alive and intact, writing about it.

I saw the children inside of them feeling hurt and scared and jealous, and acting out at me. I saw my child inside feeling hurt, scared, jealous, and acting out at them too.

It's not that I didn't have a right to be angry, to feel legitimate disappointment and rage. Because I did. There is no comforting illusion rising up to color what happened in a rosy bright light. It is as dark as my pain perceived it to be.

But the abuse and neglect were like a big black storm cloud I had just passed through. Looking back, I could still see the pelting rain and lightening flashes and hear the thunder roll. What was subtly, yet remarkably, different was to observe it from a place beyond. Finally, I wasn't right in the middle, being dumped on and feeling torn asunder. I was watching it as if it were behind me, at long last.

My mind wondered: is this what forgiveness is **really** about? Not that sappy giving in I had always imagined, that syrupy sweetness purring out of a cherubic little girl saying "it's all right" and meaning it in a way I could never feel.

No, it was not like that. This was more like a gentle moving onward to a different place, one at a distance from the old pain. It was apparent that freeing up the buried neediness was what had generated the movement. I acknowledged the pain but I did not cling. It was in a place now where letting go was a real possibility. I was free to make my own choice.

I knew I had loved my family before. I had loved them even when they did not love me. I had dearly hoped for their acceptance and approval and now that hope was dead. Would I choose to be closed or open in the future? I saw that, actually, I had not two but three alternatives.

One was to be closed and hateful, clinging to negative pictures. They were pictures that had validity and were supported by evidence, pictures that would go on feeding my perfectly legitimate rage.

The trouble was: the rage was gone. I did not feel it anymore. It had melted away like the wicked witch of the west leaving a puddle on the floor. All that was left was compassion for what we had suffered and a deep enduring sadness.

Two was to be open and, imbued with new understanding, to come back to the family hoping for something better, something that would break through the old dynamics and generate connection.

I am reminded of a story Ram Dass told about his relationship with his father. The gulf of misunderstanding between this old Jewish business man in New York and his weirdly dressed spiritual son was immense. His father wished Ram Dass could be "successful" like his brother, the wealthy insurance salesman. Little did he know that this son he found disappointing was actually a world famous teacher and guru who brought East Indian thought to the West.

Nor did Ram Dass have any illusions that his aging father could come to see who he was or ever understand what his life was about. That was impossible. But he still wanted some closeness with him. The answer he found was: YAHTZEE. His father loved the game so Ram Dass played it with him. For hours. They found their bonding and closeness and comraderie in playing Yahtzee together.

Was there a "Yahtzee" that would work for me? Maybe so but I didn't see it. I knew that for me, being open meant being hurt. Anything I did got twisted and sent back to me as a failure on my part. Even a phone call with my mother flung me into depression for weeks. I did not have the spiritual loftiness of Ram Dass. My ego was easily crushed. I needed every ounce of energy I could muster to be there for my sons. I was not angry but I could not be open. I had to save myself or what was left of myself after the loss of my partner and my family. I had to let go.

Three was to see the truth and move on – as if they were the chrysalis and I had become a butterfly.

I just gave up. I gave up trying. I gave up hoping. I gave up contact. I wrote a last letter to my mother extolling her for every conceivable contribution I could possibly credit her with. I exaggerated her positives and never made mention of how badly she had let me down. I wished her the best in every way. In the end she died without leaving a word for me, not a message of forgiveness or of love. Just nothing.

We need to hold positive pictures while still remembering the negative ones – there, in the background as a perpetual reminder, much like ballast – of the unalterably dual nature of the human being.

Thus moves the dance of the shadow: through One, Two, Three.

* * *

In the next section, the journey will take a new turn. It is as if, in rising to the peak to look ahead, we discover a new, unanticipated twist in the road.

Part Six

Loving Self, Loving Relationships

"If I am not for myself, who will be for me?
And when I am for myself, what am 'I'?
And if not now, when?"

(Avoth 1:14).

Let us pause and take our bearings. We have come a long way. We need to assess how far we have traveled and how much we have learned on the way.

In Part One, we saw how the self becomes divided, how parts are denied and suppressed, and how, as a consequence of our interaction with others, the false self and the shadow arise. It is in the mirroring process that we first experience a demand to be *other* than we are. This demand is, in essence, an experience of pressure - both from outside and from within. We feel the pressure of other people's needs being imposed upon us at the same time as we feel the pressure of our own needs to be loved and taken care of by them.

Relationship based in neediness always has this subtle quality of pressure in it, ranging widely along a spectrum from coy and seductive manipulation to extreme and blatant use of force. We call this need-driven way of relating *fusion*. It operates out of a basic assumption that others are there for the satisfaction of our needs and that we, therefore, have a right to put pressure on them to satisfy us. As a mode of interacting, fusion is not a being *with*, but an acting upon. In opposition to love, it does not accept the other as they are but places demands on the other to be as we want them to be.

In Part Two, we followed the dynamics of fusion into the arena of ordinary human relationships, particularly those of the family. We drew the chilling conclusion that much of what passes as normal everyday interaction is, in fact, abusive. Without realizing it, we are caught in a cycle of abuse that moves through time from one generation to the next and, at a given time, from one relationship to another. We are, therefore, unconscious participants in emotionally abusive relationships a large percentage of the time. Its invisibility fosters the perpetuation of abuse. The more we expose the dynamic of victim/abuser interaction, the more likelihood we will have of stepping out of it.

What we have learned from others becomes internalized.

The ways we have been victimized will be repeated, not only in the ways we abuse others, but also in the ways we abuse ourselves. In Part Three, we began to confront the internal abuser in the self, the Superego. It is the part inside us that puts pressure on us just as people outside us do. It criticizes and condemns, threatens and intimidates. It reiterates the demands and exhortations of those who have been closest to us in the family. In this way, it acts as a support system for the false self. As we begin to challenge the power of the Superego and to resist its tyranny over us, we loosen the constraints of this false self. We cease being dominated by an image of who we think we have to be to be loved and approved of. We become free to experience those feelings, beliefs and perceptions that were unacceptable to significant others in the past. We become free to discover who we really are.

Those parts of ourselves that were suppressed and denied as a result of our accommodation to other people's demands will become accessible, if we but have the daring to proceed. It is not easy to face a shadow part of ourselves that we have always hidden and disowned.

It is possible to respond to other people's demands of us with either compliance or defiance. In each case, there will be a corresponding part of ourselves that we have been forced to deny.

In Part Four, we explored the forbidden territory of anger and hatred. For those of us who have responded primarily with compliance to pressure from others, our shadow will contain all those negative feelings we were never allowed to express. Uncovering all the *no's* behind our *yes's*, all the rage behind our smiles, begins to dissolve the frozen mask of niceness which had us locked in the victim role. By releasing all this fierce negative energy, we become empowered to set limits and to act on our own behalf. We break out of depression. We become advocates for ourselves. We are no longer waiting for rescue from the ideal parent we always wished for and never had.

In Part Five, we confronted our neediness. For those of us who have responded primarily with defiance to the pressure of other people's demands, the most abhorrent part of ourselves will be our own neediness. Suddenly our strength collapses. Our cocky threats are so much hot air. We realize that, in fact, we cannot make it on our own as we had always assumed, without our health, our professional image, or our loved ones there. In this devastating experience is a glimpse of our disenchantment with relationship from a much earlier time, a disappointment so deep that we could never wholly trust again. We see our brokenness; we feel the wound we have never recovered from. It is a humbling experience, one that subdues our will and deflates our arrogance. Behind our facade of adulthood, we *are* the howling infant, the clingy, desperate child.

Face to face with the neediness inside, will we turn away in scorn and contempt? Will we clamp our hands over our ears to shut out the cries? Will we explode in anger and rage? Will we scream at the child? The way we are immediately inclined to react is an imprint of the way we were treated before or, at least, of what we internalized from the way we were treated before. Self-criticism and self-denial are inner voices from the past. Our self-abuse is a *learned* reaction.

Fortunately, it is possible to learn a new way of responding to ourselves, a compassionate and supportive way. By becoming a sympathetic witness, we can break away from the reenactment of the past. We can become, for ourselves, the parent we have been wishing for.

This is not an easy learning. Would that these processes unfolded in the self in neat succession the way a book unfolds, one part after another, in an irreversible forward direction. In the self, the parts intermingle. They slip around and do not hold an order. We may be spraying up anger from a compliant reaction at the same time as we are collapsing into neediness from a defiant reaction and still, at the same time, fighting messages from the Superego that we should not be either angry *or* weak. Of course, we are both. It is important to remember that compliance and defiance coexist in each of us, although, depending on our style of relating, one may be overt while the other is covert.

Some of us swing from one extreme to the other, placating until we become fearful of losing ourselves and then stubbornly withdrawing into ourselves until we become fearful of losing connection with other people.

At the one extreme, we meet the *fear of engulfment.* We worry: will I lose myself? Will I be controlled? Will I become an appendage, a mere reflection of the other?

At the opposite extreme is the *fear of abandonment.* Now we worry: will you reject me? Will I be unloved? Will I be all alone? The perpetual vacillation between these two extremes creates the struggle of relationship.

*   *   *

IMAGINARY DIALOGUE

She: To keep one's heart open when one is rejected is either the greatest lunacy or the greatest love. The crunch is in not knowing which.

He: I know you feel rejected but which one of us did the rejecting is not altogether clear.

She: What do you mean?

He: We have different pictures of what happened and of who did what to whom.

She: Yes, and our pictures are so wildly different! Can two pictures be more opposite? More self-contained and mutually exclusive? What is the truth then?

He: Truth! You're always looking for truth! Whose truth? You operate inside your bubble and I in mine. You deal with the dramas called out by events in the here and now inside your own bubble, events which are felt, perceived, and understood through the template of your own past unresolved issues. I am in my own bubble, acting out of and reacting to my own past dramas.

She: If we're each in our own bubble, when do we meet?

He: Good question. I tried to tell you it was a rare occurrence, our meeting, and yet all-powerful. I don't know how much you ever saw of me as I know myself.

She: Or you me. I could hardly recognize myself in your picture of me. It was so black. I know I never thought half the things you thought I thought. Nor intended, nor planned, nor even wanted what came about.

He: No more than I! Do you think I saw myself the way you saw me? Your vision horrified me. Neither of us could bear the reflection of ourselves in the mirror of the other.

She: That sounds like shadow stuff. Maybe we each saw in the other what the other unconsciously denied and then hated the other for seeing it.

He: Or projected on the other what we unconsciously denied in ourselves.

She: Or surfaced in each other our own shadow self.

He: It sounds like the unconscious was doing more in this relationship than we were! Wasn't it Albert Ellis who said of the mystery of relationship that a man finds a woman whose holes in her head match exactly the rocks in his?

She: I guess we were well matched then! I remember the moment I met you like a scene from a Harlequin romance or a 50's movie. I was walking into the Counseling Psych building where the advanced clinical hypnosis workshop was about to begin, grasping my blue sheet of directions anxiously in my hand. You spoke to me and everything stopped for a moment and went luminous. I know how soapy this sounds but that's what happened.

You kept on walking and I lined up at the registration desk, smiling and chatting to the woman   next   to me as if nothing unusual was happening while all the time a voice in my head was announcing prophetically: "THIS IS A MOMENT OF CHOICE FOR YOU! A MOMENT WHEN DESTINY PARTS THE CURTAINS AND SHOWS YOU A GLIMPSE OF A PATH THAT IS YOURS IF YOU BUT CHOOSE TO FOLLOW IT!" Not the sort of voice I hear every day! What unconscious forces were at play then? What unknown power recognized in you a co-player in some cosmic dance? . . . a figure from a past life? . . . a neurotic with an exactly matching pathology?

He: For me, it was when we did hypnosis together and took each other down to that underground cavern and swam together - that was the moment something deep was aroused in me.

She: Hah! We know where you were coming from!

He: C'mon now, men can be romantic too! We're not just neolithic gonads on the march! I would have liked to dismiss you as merely a sexual attraction and I tried, you know I did, but it didn't work. Maybe we were in a mutual hypnotic spell for years, prisoners of our own extraordinary skills as hypnotists.

She: We were certainly prisoners of our own expectations of the other, caught up in a mutual fusion in which each of us tried to force the other to be what we wanted them to be.

He: I told you that. You wouldn't listen to me.

She: It's funny. Since we've been apart, I've noticed frequently that, in areas of disagreement between us, I've come to occupy your point of view - now that I am free to draw my own conclusions without pressure from you. I guess you know what I mean about pressure . . .?

He: With a vengeance! You were so dictatorial and you

always had some ultimatum to force your way.

She: But in the end, I hardly ever got my way! You would make an agreement. Then you'd change your mind and do what you wanted anyway — even when it meant breaking promises or breaking contracts or leaving me in the lurch.

He: Uh, oh! Here we go again! The power and control game. Killer tennis.

She: I don't think I could have seen a way out of that game until I discovered my own power, but it was so different from the power I was looking for. I had to learn how to stand behind myself. Not how to take a stand on the outside - I was good at that - but how to feel truly okay about myself on the inside. To accept that what I think and perceive and feel is valid even when it differs radically from what others think or see or want to hear. I had to face how difficult that is for me.

He: We're back in the bubbles again, our own separate takes on reality. Maybe when you secretly doubted yourself, you put all the more pressure on me to agree with you. But I had trouble standing behind myself too. I had to learn to say no and stick to it.

She: But isn't that defiance? A reactive "no"? A fear of losing yourself or a fear of being controlled?

He: I guess that's up to me to decide, huh?

She: You're right. I almost slipped into it again, trying to get you to buy into my interpretation of you when I was just saying how important it is to hold my own view. This power and control stuff is insidious.

He: And yet simple. If I am me, how can I lose me? What is there to fear?

She: I remember a story Ram Dass told about a little boy who was chased up a tree by an older, bigger boy. As the second boy began climbing the tree after the first, the little boy called out: "I made you climb this tree!" After a moment's hesitation, the bigger boy climbed down the tree and began to walk away, pursued by the jeering of the boy up the tree who cried out: "I made you climb down from this tree! I made you walk away! Everything in your life from this moment on, I made you do!"

He: Isn't that like your putting me in this book and making me speak your lines? Treating me as though I'm in your mind: a projection,   an illusion, or a memory. The person you knew would never stick around in your bubble. I'm outa here!

She: What is there beyond power and control? Beyond projection of unmet child needs? Beyond us in our separate bubbles? Perhaps there are just the moments when my heart opens and I know without inhibition, contraction or fear, wholly and with all of me, that I love. Even if I love an illusion. Even if I love a projection. Even if I love a person who does not love me. I love, therefore, I am. Logic or lunacy.

* * *

Power struggles in general, and marital conflict in particular, can be illuminated by looking at the patterns of compliance and defiance in intimate relationships. Let us consider some examples.

Bea is afraid of Morris's anger so she "walks on eggshells" around him. He sees that she is being placating and doesn't trust her. He suspects that she speaks against him behind his back. In fact, she does. She complains about him to their children and gets them to side with her against him.

Doris spends years complaining about how miserable she is living with her husband Bert and how happy she would be without him. Then Bert leaves her for another woman. Doris spends years complaining about how miserable she is without

Bert and how happy she would be if he came back.

Jean is terrified that Rick will leave her so she keeps him on a short rein. She insists that he call her from work several times a day and she gets very upset if he is even a few minutes late coming home. When he goes out of town on business, she calls to check up on him at night and interrogates him about every minute of his day. Rick gets tired of being treated like a little boy and resolves to leave her.

Mark admires Carrie's spirited independence, her spontaneity in following her own impulses. He wishes he was more like her. Then, when he marries her, he is indignant that she goes off on her own without consulting him. He criticizes her for being a thoughtless and inconsiderate partner.

Martin is contemptuous of his wife Jane because she is "just a housewife" and has no interests of her own. When Jane wants to set up a business, Martin refuses to finance it, arguing that she lacks the requisite experience to be successful. When Jane finds a job, he complains bitterly about her lack of attention to the household. He makes jokes about her measly salary and her being tired every night. He says he wishes he had a wife who was an equal to him.

Bill and Barbara never fight. They always try to please each other and to get along at all cost. They do everything together and they are always smiling and affectionate. They appear to be the perfect couple, even to themselves. The only problem is, they have not had sex for years. It is a shock to everybody when they separate.

David and Melanie are madly in love. They want to spend all their time together and they can barely tear themselves apart. They gaze into each other's eyes in endless fascination.

Then they have a fight. They fly apart in rage and fury. They scream insults at each other and neither will relent. They walk away; they don't speak; they don't see each other for a while. Then the need comes up again, the missing, the insatiable longing. They fly back together with the same passionate intensity and are glued together until the fighting starts again. This goes on for years and years. It is "true love," they say.

Like David and Melanie, we frequently confuse neediness and love. This is a simple and, at the same time, extraordinarily difficult distinction. We may understand it intellectually, but we do not live by it. All these vignettes as well as countless others like them are evidence of our deep-seated confusion. The truth is: our compliance and defiance, our dependence and counter-dependence, our jealousy and envy are all impelled by neediness, not by love. To grasp the profound significance of this distinction, we need to assimilate each of the following critical facets of the truth:

1. Love arises out of fullness; it is an experience of expansion. Neediness arises out of deficiency; it is an experience of contraction.

2. Love and neediness, though distinct, can arise together. When I love you, I appreciate you as you are. When I need you, I require that you be a certain way.

3. The intensity of my need for you is proof, not of how much I love you, but of how much I need to be loved.

4. The less I felt loved as a child, the more intense will be my need for love.

5. The experience of love triggers our old wounds. We re-experience the anger, hatred, and pain caused by the

frustration of our needs as a child. Thus, we most often become hateful to those we love.

6. When we are frustrated in our need for love, we become cut off from our own experience of love. It is not only the disconnection from the love of others but also the disconnection from our own love that creates such a deep wound in us.

7. Hatred is generated by frustrated love. We learn to hate not only other people but also, at the deepest level, ourselves.

8. We turn to others in the hope of making up for the love we have lost within ourselves. This false hope fuels our neediness.

9. How we respond to the neediness in ourselves will have a direct bearing on our capacity to love ourselves.

10. We must learn to love ourselves *before* we can be genuinely open to loving or being loved by another. Love of self is not the consequence but the starting point.

If only it were not so difficult to love ourselves! It seems as if it should be easy but it's not. It is an inordinately difficult task and, the more we need to do it, the more difficult it seems to be.

From one vantage point, all psychotherapy can be seen, in essence, as an attempt, through a loving therapeutic bond, to help a person learn to love themselves. What makes the therapy process so deeply challenging, as we have seen, are the roadblocks in the way, obstacles as formidable as silencing the Superego and wrestling with the Shadow. At this juncture, is there anything more we can offer to guide us on our way to help in the task of opening our hearts to love?

The injunction to love oneself will immediately set off cries of "selfishness!" and "self-indulgence!" from outside the self as well as from within. Most of us believe that love of self is the same as selfishness. Since we have been socialized to condemn selfishness, we reject love of self. Our fear is that if we learn to love ourselves, we will be hateful to others. In fact, the opposite is more often the case. We are most likely to be hateful when we do *not* love ourselves and most likely to be loving when we *do*.

However, it is absolutely crucial, as we said before, that we distinguish between *feeling* all our feelings and *acting them out*. We need to accept our hateful feelings and to earnestly follow them back to their source. But that does not mean we have permission to act out our hate. Abusive treatment is unacceptable whether we are the perpetrators or the recipients. The more we love ourselves, the less willing we are to be treated abusively. We cannot fail to acknowledge that the same principle must be applied to others as we apply to ourselves. The principle of universality is the foundation, the *sine qua non*, of morality.[71]

Contrary to our preconceptions, self-love is not in conflict with this principle. In fact, it makes it easier for us to live in a moral way. The more we love ourselves, the more we can contain all feelings, of whatever sort, within a loving acceptance of self and explore them without exploding in reaction. Thus, the more we love ourselves, the more we will be able to feel our malice toward others without acting it out.

Self-love helps us to protect ourselves so that we do not fall into victim-abuser interactions on *either* side of the pendulum swing. It teaches us to care for and take care of ourselves at the same time. It moves us toward the satisfaction of our needs. Out of satisfaction and fullness, we are able to give to others; out of frustration and emptiness, we become desperate

---

71 See, for example, Kant, Immanuel: *Foundations of the Metaphysics of Morals*, (translated by L.W. Beck), Indiapolis, 1970.

to receive. We are convinced that we need what others have because we don't think we have "enough." We are seeking outside what is missing within. Thus, our fighting, our power and control, our domination and submission, all stem from a sense of deficiency. Like Mother Hubbard, we are going to a cupboard that is bare. We need to stock our larders and feed ourselves on generous helpings of self-care, self-validation and self-acceptance before we will be able to share.

We begin in simple ways. We attend to our needs. We learn to enjoy life and to have fun. Instead of being self-punitive, we are gentle and nurturing to ourselves. We listen to the child within. We practice honoring all our feelings, trusting that whatever we feel is okay, although, as we have said repeatedly, what we *do* is another matter.

Being self-indulgent is a good way of fostering loving acceptance of self so long as we take care that what is nurturing to self is not abusive to others. We want to cease being in either the victim or the abuser role. We learn to say no without attacking ourselves, feeling guilty, blowing up, or closing off. We use the anger won from shadow work as strength to protect ourselves. We use the neediness as humility to open us to face the truth. It softens our defenses and helps us manage the pain that facing the truth will bring.

If we begin to practice loving ourselves, we will find out all too quickly that there are those in our circle of relationships who will support us and those who will not. Making allowance for our fumbling efforts, what will become sadly apparent is how frequently we meet resistance and all-out attempts at sabotage.

The sad truth is that those we love do not always want us to love ourselves. They may equate self-love with selfishness and be motivated by the misguided fear that they will lose out. They may be clinging to familiar patterns and the fear of what is new. The last and most distressing possibility is they may be people who, though we love them, are *not* on our side.

The fact is that when we do not love ourselves, we often attract people into our lives who reinforce our negative self-image and play out the roles of those who gave us this poor self-image in the first place. Sometimes learning to love ourselves may require us to cut the ties that would keep us mired in self-hate. We may need to reverse the question asked in the title of a popular book on marital therapy *Do I Have to Give Up Me to Be Loved by You?* [72] and ask instead " Do I Have to Give Up You to be Loved by Me?" After all else is tried, the final litmus test is:

Does this relationship make me feel better or worse about myself?

Sometimes we may not like the answer we receive.

* * *

Lady of Love

When she arrived, she always made a grand entrance. She'd come in as if she were riding on a huge breaking wave. Her brilliant smile was like a beacon light to guide her as she sailed her multi-colored shawl through the doorway.

"Helloooooo! Helloooooo!" she'd croon in her melodious foreign accent as her crested wave swept upon the shore. "Helloooooo! Here I am! And how are you all?" Her words of greeting foamed and bubbled all around us. She'd wag her head approvingly in all directions, darting glances like sunbeams bouncing off the sea. The air was aglow with reassurance. We all knew our teacher had arrived.

She held out love like a warm promise. When she spoke, she gushed. We were buoyed up by that uplifting feeling. Would her radiance enlighten us? She had soaked in the most illustrious learning and she was certainly eager to pass that learning on to us.

---

72 Paul, Jordan and Margaret: *Do I Have to Give Up Me to be Loved By You?*
CompCare Publishers, Minneapolis, Minnesota, 1983.

She assured us that the way was simple and soon we would know it too. After years of thirsting in the desert, had we reached the lush oasis at last? There was an in-held breath of longing in the room.

She was poetic and inspiring as a teacher, erudite yet in a meat-and-potatoes kind of way. Her teaching fit nicely with what I knew already but it beckoned me to take a step beyond. Quietly I was transported to a higher level. Her vision gave my understanding wings. As my mind absorbed her therapeutic style of healing, on a deeper level my soul was becoming spiritualized.

She was my teacher, my therapist, my guide. I slid gratefully into an idolizing stance. It all moved so quickly and so beautifully. Within a few short months, I was teaching at her side! Imagine my delight as I was transformed from client to colleague, from eager student to equal partner with her. I had the logic her intuition cried out for, the analytic clarity her lofty vision craved. I was in no way a minor player in the course we taught together. On the contrary, I took on the lion's share. Though it was obvious that the contribution I was making was major, I seemed unable to grasp the truth that our success was equally because of me. In my eyes, she was the star. How easy it was to see my flaws and her virtues! In reality, we made a very effective team.

The sad fate of such illusions is inevitable. Once again, I discovered that stars may become street lamps. She taught me about the victim/abuser dynamic and then she enacted her teaching for me. When I slid into victim position, she metamorphosed into abuser instantly.

Perhaps she could not bear her quick descent from stardom. I watched, aghast, as the hatred came up in her, this lady of love. Her benevolence transformed into malevolence before my astonished eyes. Such is the power of idealization that it makes us blind, deaf, and (remarkably) dumb. She said I reminded her of her mother and that was clearly a person she did not want to see. Without informing me, she went behind my back and cancelled the workshop we had prepared to give together and set up one for her to give alone. I was devastated when I found out.

While I was still reeling in the after-shock, she called me up and cheerfully remarked to me: "I'm sorry that you are so deeply distressed, but I have to say that I am not at all feeling that way." Her tone was buoyant and magnanimous. "Goody for you" I was thinking to myself. Then in a most cordial manner, she invited me to meet her for lunch "to celebrate the goodness of our relationship." To my credit and to her consternation, I declined.

* * *

In order to overcome the influence of non-supportive relationships and to help nourish a positive sense of self, I sometimes work with affirmations. I will describe my methodology so that, if you wish, you can use them too.

Affirmations are positive statements made in the present about the future as if it were past. That is, they express the way we would *like* to be as if it were already a confirmed reality and as if, having been a reality for some time, it had become the way we readily saw ourselves. In this way, affirmations mirror back to us the self we would become if we loved ourselves and were enabled to develop in the nurturing context of that love. Paradoxically, then, they mirror the self we will become if we become who we truly are.

What makes it difficult to become our true selves is, as we have seen, our abandonment of ourselves in response to other people's needs. We adopt false pictures of who we are and who we need to be. Because of the deeply ingrained power of these old learnings, we have to take an active role in reshaping our sense of self. Affirmations are one way of doing our reshaping work.

There are many good books on affirmations.[73] My only reservation about using such books is that, in my view, it is vital to formulate, or, I would prefer to say, "birth," an affirmation oneself rather than to choose one from a pre-selected list.

---

73 Two examples of many are the writings of Sondra Ray, *I Deserve Love: How Affirmations Can Guide You to Personal Fulfillment*, Celestial Arts, Berkeley, California, 1976 or Shakti Gawain, *Reflections in the Light: Daily Thoughts and Affirmations*, New World Library, San Rafael, California, 1988.

If the affirmation is to be an expression of who you deeply are, then it can only come from you yourself. The process of developing our own affirmations is an important part of the reshaping work.

To illustrate, perhaps you are struggling with a particular negative message, say, for example, that you are lazy, stupid or cowardly. As a first step, imagine how you would feel and act if this were *not* so. Get as vivid and detailed a picture as you can by playing out in your imagination a variety of different scenes. If you have trouble picturing yourself in the way you desire, imagine someone that you deeply admire or respect who exemplifies the qualities that you aspire to possess. Again, see that person operating in an assortment of different situations that are relevant to your life.

Now make a list of adjectives or brief adjectival phrases describing yourself (or the person who is acting as your projection screen) in terms of the way you feel (or they appear) in these scenes. Keep on generating adjectives, without editing, until your list runs dry.

For example, a client who wanted to be more confident in social situations saw herself at a party she had recently attended. Instead of sitting silently by herself as she had done, she imagined herself milling around, smiling and chatting comfortably with everyone. She got in touch with how she felt in this new role and how others at the party responded to her. Then she visualized other situations in her life in which she saw herself behaving in a more outgoing and sociable manner. She described herself this way:

happy	carefree	spontaneous	uninhibited
unselfconscious	free	easy-going	cheerful
talkative	well-liked	light	fluid
natural	relaxed	happy to be me	flowing
proud	assertive	out-front	confident
sociable	pleasant	cordial	popular
comfortable			

When your list of adjectives is complete, go through it several times, eliminating all those adjectives that seem redundant or derivative. Choose the quintessential qualities that encapsulate this desired state of being for you. Keep crossing off items until there are just three or four adjectives left on the list. These will be the core ingredients of your affirmation.

For my client, they were:

happy to be me   light   free-flowing

As a next step, these qualities will need to be ordered in a first-person sentence in the present tense. Consider all combinations and permutations of these terms until you find the order that is right for you. You need to be sensitive to sound, to feel, and to meaning. You can think of the first term as the spring-board or starting point, the second as the conduit, and the third as the final expression or result of this state of being. Include yourself (i.e. your name) in the statement.

My client chose as her affirmation:

I, Tracy, am light, free-flowing, and happy to be me.

The standard form of integrating the message of an affirmation is to write it a certain number of times - say 30 to 50 times - every day for several weeks. It is the repetition on a daily basis that is essential for changing our habitual modes of viewing ourselves.

Beyond repetition, there is another factor that is important to consider here. The act of writing is particularly effective because it involves the cooperation of both visual and motor systems, therefore giving us feedback from two different types of sensory cues. But once we have acknowledged the power of combining different sensory modalities, why stop with writing?

What makes more sense is to move in a multi-media direction in working with affirmations rather than limiting our effectiveness by simply following the standard practice of writing each day. Thus a better approach is to experience affirmations through as many different sensory modalities as our imaginations will allow. Here are some of my suggestions:

(1) Repeat your affirmation into a tape-recorder experimenting with different subtleties of meaning that are associated with placing the emphasis on different words eg:

I, Tracy, am *light,* free-flowing, and happy to be me.
I, Tracy, am light, *free-flowing,* and happy to be me.
I, Tracy, am light, free-flowing, and *happy* to be me.
I, Tracy, am light, free-flowing, and happy to be *me.*

or changing the rhythms and cadences of your speech:

I, Tracy, am light . . . . free-flowing, and happy to be me.
I, Tracy, am light, free-flowing . . . . . and happy to be me.
I, Tracy, am light, free . . . . . flowing, and happy . . . . . to be . . . . me.

or changing the person from how we see ourselves (first) to what another says to us (second) to what we appear to others to be (third):

I, Tracy, am light, free-flowing, and happy to be me.
Tracy, you are light, free-flowing, and happy to be you.
Tracy is light, free-flowing, and happy to be herself.

(2) Listen to the tape or let it play in the background

while you drive, dress, eat, and do your laundry.

(3) Repeat the affirmation over and over to yourself in your head like a mantra while you are doing other things.

(4) Walk in time to the beat of your affirmation.

(5) Dance to it.

(6) Sing it in the shower, in the kitchen, in the car.

(7) Whistle to it.

(8) Drum it.

(9) Say it to yourself in the mirror several times a day.

(10) Put yourself into a deep hypnotic state and repeat the affirmation every day. You may use silent abreaction[74] to facilitate acceptance of this new image of yourself.

This brings us to a last critical point: the use of hypnosis. In my view, hypnotic suggestion is as powerful as writing and should be included in your practice every day. Using hypnosis adds a new dimension to working with an affirmation in that it directly addresses the unconscious mind and elicits its support. If the unconscious is not a willing participant in your endeavor, transformation will be, at best, tenuous and, at worst, blocked. You may learn something about the response of your unconscious mind by paying attention to your dreams.

Eg. Tracy had a dream in which she was a seagull, blissfully flying in the sky, carried by warm currents of air, swooping and hovering with ease. Obviously, her unconscious mind was pleased.

Affirmations are one way to nurture the self with loving

74 See above, Part Four, page 132.

words. It is also helpful to develop a personal gesture of self-soothing such as patting or stroking your chest or putting your arms around yourself, in combination with words of reassurance such as you would say to a child. My friend Tanya, for example, learned to pat her chest and repeat softly to herself, "There, there, it's okay — I love you, no matter what." I teach this technique to clients as "Tanya's tom-tom." Gestures of this sort convey a direct message of self-love. They announce that we are here as sympathetic witnesses who are willing to stand behind ourselves and beat our own drum.

But we need not stop there. Virtually any way that we can find to surround ourselves with self-enhancing messages, self-caring activities, or nurturing experiences will be beneficial in developing our love of self, repairing the damage from past hurts, and restoring our sense of self when we lose it, as we often do. It is important to develop a list of experiences that can serve this function, especially for those times when we feel disconnected and depressed. One client called this her "Sunshine List." Because each of us is different, our lists will be different but because we are also similar, these ideas from another sunshine list may be inspiring to you.

A Sunshine List

* Walk along the beach.
* Soak in a hot bath with candles burning and classical music playing.
* Make yourself chicken soup or a cup of tea, depending on your ethnic leaning.
* Choose a romantic card and send it to yourself.
* Take a mental health day and stay home from work.
* Play with your dog or cat.
* Go for a drive without a predetermined destination.
* Curl up in a comfort blanket with a stuffed animal and suck your thumb or just hug yourself.
* Watch gulls fly.

* Give yourself a long-stemmed red rose.
* Go to bed early in cozy pajamas with your favorite
    book.
* Eat something deliciously decadent (like Häagen Dazs
    ice cream) very slowly, relishing every spoonful.
* Call up your best friend.
* Take a walk in the woods.
* Float on an air mattress.
* Watch children playing in a playground.
* Dig in the garden.
* Get a massage or a facial or a manicure.
* Make a picnic lunch on the grass.
* Put on earphones and get lost in your favorite music.
* Buy yourself a little treat.
* Write in your journal.
* Meditate.
* Plan something that you can look forward to,
    for example, a trip.
* Paint a picture
* Have a satisfying sexual experience.
* Go for a bike ride or a jog.
* Get a video or go to a movie that you've been wanting
    to see.
* Take yourself out to dinner.
* Do self-hypnosis and take yourself to a special place
    where you feel serene.

Activities of this sort rejuvenate and restore us. They bring
us back to life with renewed vigor and enthusiasm. They are
like a first-aid kit for the soul.

To test how well we are doing with our practice of self-
love, I propose the following "Ultimate Challenge" which I
have borrowed from Ram Dass:[75]

---

75 Ram Dass: "Tuning to the Wisdom Heart: Spiritual Ground for Effective Living," a
workshop at Breitenbush Retreat and Conference Centre, Detroit, Oregon, August 1993.

Suppose you were to warmly approach a person you like and were delighted to see. And suppose this person were to respond by shouting "Get away from me! You disgust me! I don't want anything to do with you!" Would you have the presence to reply: "I'm sorry you feel this way, because I really like myself and I would have liked to be close to you. But I see you need space right now so I will back off and give it to you."

If we can love ourselves in the face of rejection, even in the hideous face of other people's hate, then we can meet the challenge of love. In full comprehension of the difficulty of this task, Ram Dass remarked: "Who did you **think** you were supposed to love?"

* * *

On a particularly grim day when the world looked black and therapy work was particularly hard, I began wondering what else I might do. The thought occurred to me that I could become a T-shirt author composing clever captions for the T-shirt industry. Instead of doing therapy, I could distribute my own line of avant-garde, therapeutically correct T-shirts for sale at workshops, conferences and retreats.

One of them would definitely be: "KEEP ON SUCKING" with a picture of an enormous thumb.

Here are some of my other favorite captions:

THE TRUTH SHALL MAKE YOU FREE ...
 But first it shall make you miserable.

I WANT TO BE WHATEVER I CHOOSE ...
 Even if my mother approves.

*WHO DID YOU **THINK** YOU WOULD BE LIKE???*

GO HAVE YOUR ABANDONMENT CRISIS
   BY YOURSELF!!!

PAIN HURTS and ABUSE is ABUSIVE

THE GREAT ICK

YOU NEED INFORMATION??? Dial 4 -1 -1

WHY DO I ALWAYS IMAGINE THERE IS
   SOMEONE WITH **MORE SENIORITY?**

THAT WAS IT!

I DON'T DO **RELATIONSHIPS!**

I GAVE AT THE OFFICE

DO I HAVE TO GIVE UP YOU TO BE LOVED
   BY ME?

WHO DID YOU **THINK** YOU WERE SUPPOSED
   TO LOVE??

*It is ironic to realize that I would then fulfill a popular cultural
stereotype by making my fortune in the garment industry.*

* * *

Once we have learned to love ourselves, we cannot help
but notice that there are other folks out there who deserve to
be treated similarly. From the vantage point of self-love, we
come to the arena of relationship with changed expectations.
We no longer look to the other to be, as Virginia Satir used to
say, "the window dressing to our validity." We take charge of
our own sense of self, our own self-worth. How we treat others

and how they treat us become the key issues of relationship.

There are several systems of marital therapy in use today, the most comprehensive of which is the *P.A.I.R.S. (Practical Application of Intimate Relationship Skills)* program. You can learn about the work of P.A.I.R.S. by reading the newly published *Passage to Intimacy* [76] by Dr. Lori Gordon. It covers a wide range of issues that arise in intimate relationships and is well worth the read. The success of its techniques, as well as those of any other relationship approach, is contingent upon the maturity of the individuals involved and the extent to which they have done their own individual work. As Dr. Gordon says: "Nothing is more important to intimacy than your sense of self-worth. How you feel about yourself in relation to other people is a major factor in the quality of your intimate relationships. And trouble in a relationship almost always involves a problem with self-esteem." [77] In other words, to love another, it is necessary to love oneself first. The success of our love relationships hinges on this. Judging by the appalling divorce rate, we must conclude that we have a great deal of learning to do.

If we simply leave a marriage without coming to terms with our issues from the past, we will reenact the same issues in the next relationship. Although our new partner may look very different from the last, we will soon discover, to our deep dismay, that we are living out the same script. In this sense, *divorce won't help.* Unless we are prepared to wrestle with the demons of the past and to resolve our issues with them, we will be stuck in a repeating cycle.

The same is true within the context of a marriage. If we simply drop issues or move past them without coming to terms with our demons, we will find the same issues coming up over and over again, in an endlessly repeating cycle. Often the script is so familiar that we can predict our lines and those of our partner with deadly accuracy. Though the pain is acute, we

---

76 Gordon, Lori H.: *Passage to Intimacy*, Simon & Schuster Inc., New York, 1993.
77 Ibid., page 47.

keep acting out the same scene. However we long to escape, *avoidance won't help*. Until we break free of the stranglehold of the past, we are powerless to stop the reenactment.

The technique I keep coming back to with couples who are caught up in a reenactment cycle is the simplest, most basic exercise in communication, the "I Feel" exercise. Just as the letters of the alphabet form the building blocks of the written word, this exercise contains the building blocks of communication. Just as the letters can be used for anything from "Jump, Spot, Jump!" to the most advanced treatise, so this exercise can be used for any level of communication from the most rudimentary to the most complex. We should not be deceived by its simplicity. It can be very powerful and it can show us where we are stuck.

First I will outline the exercise and then I will comment on each step.

THE "I FEEL" EXERCISE

(1) A: I feel _____.

(2) B: Tell me about it.   OR: Not now.   How about..?
                                 A: Okay

(3) A: Well, I feel _____

    _____

(4) B: So you feel _____

    _____

(5) A: Yes   OR   Not exactly.

(6)   A: Goes Back to line(3)

(7)   B: Goes Back to line (4)

(8)   A: Goes Back to line (5)

The communication is not complete until A says Yes.
What we have here is one unit of communication - i.e. a

message sent by the speaker (A) and received by the listener (B). When the speaker confirms the accuracy of the message received, the transaction is complete. Then the listener (B) becomes the speaker (A) and the exercise repeats. Though laborious, this exercise is like a slow-motion movie of where communication breaks down and, therefore, of what is necessary to repair it. Let us see how this is so.

Line (1) is a brief statement of a feeling.
Eg. I feel annoyed, worried, sad, scared, hurt, lonely etc.

Sounds easy? But it is surprising how many people have difficulty right from the start. In order to begin the exercise, we have to know what feelings are as distinct from thoughts, beliefs and judgments and we have to be able to identify the feelings we have. Thus, line (1) presupposes a level of awareness that not everybody has.

For instance, I have often heard women bitterly complain that their husbands will not share their feelings without ever suspecting that the problem may be not so much that they will not, as that they do not know how to do so. For men and women alike, such problems are an invitation to awareness work.[78] We have to learn to recognize our feelings and to articulate them. We need familiarity with the subtle nuances of feeling and a feeling vocabulary. We need sufficient trust in ourselves and our partners that we are prepared to reveal ourselves to them. Line (1) may look easy but it is no mean accomplishment.

You will notice that line (1) is *very* short. This is deliberate. At the outset, the speaker does not have an agreement to be listened to. Some people go rattling on at great length without ever checking if their partners are willing to listen to them. Perhaps it is a bad time. Perhaps the receiver is not genuinely open to listening at that moment because they are too tired, stressed out, or preoccupied with something else.

---

78 For example, see above, Part Five, pages 165-170 on processing feelings.

It is to the benefit of both the speaker and the listener that a better time be set.

Therefore, in line (2), the listener has an option to postpone. They may say "no" for now - but not indefinitely. The onus is on the listener to propose an alternative, one that is close at hand, not twenty years hence, and to negotiate until a mutually agreeable time is set. If we know that we will have a specified time to talk, most of us can hold off and contain our feelings. If we feel brushed off or put off to the ubiquitous "later", it will be much harder to wait. Line (2) may expose those who always pick a bad time to talk or those who always complain that every time we pick is bad.

In line (2), the listener indicates their readiness to hear the other with the phrase "Tell me about it." As alternatives, "Go ahead" or "I'm ready" or "I'm willing to listen" will work. It is best to avoid *"Why?"* as a response. The "Why?" question tends to put us on the defensive; it seems to request a justification or defense rather than a clarification of what we feel.

Line (3) is noticeably longer than line (1) but it does not go on interminably. Listeners cannot take in messages that go on too long and, as a matter of fact, speakers cannot take them in either. If the situation is highly charged and conflicted, our ability to listen will decrease dramatically. According to one book on marital therapy,[79] the average time we can take in what another is saying in a conflict situation is just 14 seconds. No matter how fast we talk, we can't say much in that time!

We find out in line (4) how much the listener has actually absorbed of what has been said or, perhaps we should say, how little. It is frequently a shock to discover how difficult listening really is and how much patience and skill it takes to do it well. Certainly, it is not simply a matter of having one's ears in the room. We need caring and concentration to be able to take in and feed back what we have heard, even with the best of intentions. We may discover that, as well as having difficulty

79 Sellnor, Judith A and James G., *Loving for Life: Your self-help guide to a successful, intimate relationship*, Self-Counsel Press, Psychology Series, 2nd edition, May 1991, page 24.

listening to others, we also have trouble listening to ourselves and remembering what we have said. A good sense of humor is a definite asset in this exercise.

At the beginning level, feedback takes the form of *parroting*, that is, exact replication of what the speaker said, literally word for word. As we progress, we can move to *paraphrasing* where the meaning is conveyed in similar, though not necessarily identical, words. From there we can advance to deeper levels of listening skill, learning to empathize with the underlying meaning of what our partner feels. [80] However, the farther we stray from the original wording and the more "poetic license" we take, the higher the risk that we will distort or miss what the other is saying to us.

In line (5), the speaker will tell us how well we have done. They may need to reiterate part, or even all, of what they have said. The point here is for the speaker to feel heard by the listener, even if it means requesting numerous repetitions. Settling for less will build resentment and exacerbate the misunderstanding and mistrust that develop when we don't feel heard. It may help to remember a quip often repeated by Virginia Satir, world renowned marital and family therapist: "I may be slow but I'm *educable!*" The time we give to understanding each other communicates a message of love.

It is not necessary to agree with each other to feel loved and supported. What is essential is to feel *heard*. The "I Feel" exercise is basic training in expressing ourselves in ways that will allow us to be listened to and, as well, in listening in ways that will allow the other to feel heard. In this respect, the "I Feel" exercise trains us to be sympathetic witnesses to those who are closest in our lives. When we can share our feelings with another and listen openly to the feelings they share with us, we feel connected; we feel bonded. We open our hearts to

---

80 Based on a Rogerian model, for example, Truax has distinguished as many as eight different levels of empathic listening. See Truax, C.B., "A Scale for the Rating of Accurate Empathy" in C.R. Rogers, E.T. Gendlin, D.J. Kiesler & C.B. Truax (Eds.), *The Therapeutic Relationship and its Impact: A Study of Psychotherapy with Schizophrenics*, University of Wisconsin Press, Madison, Wisconsin, 1967.

love.

Thus, individual therapy, in conjunction with marriage and family therapy, are vehicles to support us in transcending the pain of the past and learning to love. They work with the self in the matrix of other selves or, in different terminology, the self in its object relations. They help us to address the particular events and patterns of events in our personal history that have created problems for us and they support us in dealing with these problems in a creative and constructive way. In particular, they help us disidentify with the critical voices from the past to become sympathetic witnesses to ourselves and to each other. Bonding with ourselves makes it possible for us to bond with others. And it is bonding that enables us to heal.

* * *

Am I happy now? Is this a story with a happy ending? It is a true story and what is true is that I keep on struggling. Often I slip into self-abuse and thrash around in it for a while, getting upset with myself and with others. Often I witness the victim/ abuser dance and, too often, it's myself I have to haul off the dance floor. Often I feel compassion for the suffering of others, especially for those I see close up - my clients - and I do what I can to help. When I remember the misery of the child I was, I do what I can for her too.

And at those rare times, like right now, when I remember the bliss of loving with a whole heart, I experience a deep sense of wholeness and peace and I know what I meant by **"home."**

* * *

Are we at the end of our journey? Once we have learned to love ourselves, the split begins to heal. We no longer turn against ourselves in the manner of those who abused or neglected us. We remain allied with the child. We no longer compel ourselves to be what others demand of us in the face of our own resistance. We honor our resistance and remain true to who we are. We embrace all aspects of ourselves. No parts are lopped off as unacceptable, as shadow parts. We want to include all of who we are. We want to be whole.

But *is* this all of who we are? Some voices say no. These voices coming out of the spiritual tradition argue that the self we have integrated is merely the self in relation to other selves, that is, the self in the world. They call this self the "personality" or "ego" in contradistinction from the Self with a capital "S" or spirit or soul.

The self of psychotherapy is formed in the context of relationship and requires the presence of others to exist. Even when we reintegrate the parts of ourselves that have been repressed and denied, we are still operating with parts developed out of interaction with others and defined in terms of a social world. From a psychological perspective, without the mirroring process, there would be no sense of self at all.

For example, Object Relations theory begins with the observation that the biological birth of the human infant is not the same as the psychological birth of the person. Summarizing this position as it is explicated in Margaret Mahler's seminal text, *The Psychological Birth of the Human Infant*, Almaas says:

Three points stand out in [Mahler's] statement:

1. There is no sense of a separate individual at the beginning of the life of a human being.

2. The psychological birth of an individual is a psychological achievement resulting from the separation-individuation process, in the first three years of life.

3. This development happens in the relationship to the mothering person, the primary love object; i.e., it is within the context of an object relation.[81]

The question we are immediately prompted to ask is: is

81 Almaas, A.H., *The Pearl Beyond Price: Integration of Personality into Being: An Object Relations Approach*, Diamond Books, Almaas Publications, 1988, Berkeley, California, page 23.

there a self outside the context of an object relation? If the sense we have of ourselves as individuals, separate from other people, is the result of identifying with a particular construct in the mind, is this true outside the individual mind? Can we know the answer to this question or is it impossible to know truth outside our own minds? Are we caught in what philosophers call "the egocentric predicament" or is there a way beyond the ego's limited perspective? The spiritual traditions are convinced there is a way.

Almaas explains:

> The general attitude of psychologists is to accept this ultimate lack of objectivity of the ego's perception as inevitable, although of course much of psychotherapy consists of a learning process in the patient which results in a more "realistic" perception of himself and his world. The spiritual teachings, however, claim that it is not necessary to let the ego's identification define ourselves, but that we can know ourselves more directly, in a much more real way. They claim in fact that identification with the construct of the self-image in the mind cuts us off from our true nature and from seeing the true nature of reality. [82]

This opens up a whole new realm of possibility. The spiritual perspective points beyond psychotherapy to a radically different experience of self. This is self beyond the confines of our personality, beyond the particular mirroring that occurred in our family, and beyond the limitations of self in relation to other selves. Spirituality claims to offer a way out of our private ego bubbles into the reality of being as such.

Could it be that, like the crow on that barren bluff, we are trapped in the cage of our limited conceptions? Could it be that there is a way to spread our wings and be free?

In the next section, we will venture out a little in this new direction asking: what, if anything, is beyond psychotherapy? If there is such a beyond, how are we to know?

---

82 Ibid., page 26.

Part Seven

Beyond Psychotherapy

"You have to have a self before you can see . . .
. . . you haven't got a self."

A.H. Almaas

CROW'S STORY

There is a medicine story that tells of Crow's fascination with her own shadow. She kept looking at it, scratching at it, pecking at it, until her shadow woke up and became alive. Then Crow's shadow ate her. Crow is Dead Crow now.

Dead Crow is the Left-Handed Guardian. If you look deeply into Crow's eye, you will have found the gateway to the supernatural. Crow knows the unknowable mysteries of creation and is the keeper of sacred law. [83]

* * *

We know that compliance and defiance are defensive postures; they protect the self. In order to protect the self, each of these postures shuts out an aspect of self that is threatening to that mode of defense. Compliance shuts out anger, defiance shuts out neediness. We know that we have to recognize and re-own these shadow aspects if we want to be whole.

But suppose we inquire further into what we are protecting against. Suppose we "peck and scratch" at our shadow selves, digging deeper. What is the fear behind the shadow? Is there something deeper and more threatening still?

At bottom, anger is a protest against not being loved. We were not held as we needed, not nurtured as we wanted, not accepted unconditionally as we would have liked. To a greater or lesser degree, all of us have experienced moments when we did not feel loved. What is it about such moments that are so excruciatingly painful? So terrifying? So much like touching a raw nerve?

In such moments, we feel our desperate need for love and, at the same time, the fear that it is lost. It is as if an abyss opens up before us. We feel helpless and hopeless. All support is gone. At the edge of the abyss, our anger dissolves into neediness. We need what is not there. We hang suspended in the anguish of our neediness, anxious to run away and hide, to

83 Sams, Jamie & Carson, David: *Medicine Cards: The Discovery of Power Through the Ways of Animals*, Bear & Company, Sante Fe, New Mexico, 1988, page 133.

seek comfort anywhere.

Can we allow ourselves to let go of our defenses and drop into this anguish, to experience this neediness instead of running away? For our whole lives we have been bracing ourselves against this experience, holding on with every strategy we could devise. Our personality is structured to avoid this experience, this abyss at the centre of the self. How can we loosen our hold when it seems to be our lifeline, our only means to survive? Every fiber of our known being protests against letting go. We feel certain we will be destroyed. It is by no means easy to make ourselves step over the edge.

Almaas comments:

> It is not easy to look clearly and sincerely at ourselves. Most of us don't even know what is difficult about it. We just find our minds dodging in all directions to avoid it. I break up with my boyfriend, and suddenly I'm eating. If I'm not eating, I'm doing my paintings that I haven't touched in ten years ... Our minds are clever at avoiding the feeling that arises at the end of anything, because there is a terror of having no supporting mirrors to give us meaning. Just to exist as we are brings up a big fear of the emptiness. There is usually a fear that we don't really have any Essence, and that we don't have an identity. We may believe that the emptiness is all there is.[84]

In its raw form, neediness feels like an emptiness, a deficiency, a lack. It is a void inside us around which our entire body is contracted from the clenching of fist, sphincter, teeth or jaw at the muscular level to the infinitely subtle, almost imperceptible, yet all-pervasive tension at the cellular level. This tension is coextensive with our experience of ourselves as an individual body, separate from all other bodies, occupying a particular position in space. The internal core of this individual body, this contraction in space, is the emptiness we fear and resist. It is felt as a yearning, an aching, a longing.

84 Almaas, A.H.: *Diamond Heart Book Three: Being and the Meaning of Life*, Diamond Books, Almaas Publications, Berkeley, California, 1990, page 42.

It is voiced as a wailing, a moaning, a howling. It is as if the words that we cried out to the universe were "I need! I need! I need!"

What is it that we all need and long for? If we do not shrink from the truth, our neediness calls out: "Feed me!" "Take care of me!" "Hold me!" "Tell me I matter!" Whether we plead or we rage, the essential message of our neediness is: "Love me!" "Please love me!" "I need to be loved!"

This yearning to be loved is universal. However, what we discover is that, despite our very best efforts, we do not have the capacity to compel other people to love us. Ultimately, we do not have the capacity to control other people at all.

Once we have registered the truth of our powerlessness to control anybody outside ourselves, it may dawn on us that we have, at best, limited ability to control even our own selves ‑ i.e. our own bodies or feelings or thoughts or behavior. We are vulnerable to disease, to accidents and to natural disasters. We suffer and, ultimately, we all will die. We succumb to addictions; we repeat negative patterns; we do what we know is bad for us, over and over again.

No matter how we strive for perfection, we fall short. We make mistakes, we have shortcomings, we are flawed. Sometimes we are hateful on purpose; we act out of malice and a desire for revenge. Sometimes we want to be kind but we are thoughtless; we want to be loving but we are cruel.

Faced with our own undeniable deficiencies, we may become convinced that we do not deserve to be loved at all. Alternatively, if we focus on the deficiencies of others, we will have no scarcity of examples of human insensitivity, malevolence and corruption. The reality of human evil stares us in the face. When our idealizations break down, our hate and anger are released. We hate ourselves, we hate others, and, ultimately, we hate both. The universe becomes a dark uncertain place.

* * *

July 1962. I was twenty years old when I had this experience and wrote about it, but I never showed this story to anyone before.

A Taste of Honey

The door banged shut and she was on the street. Standing, waiting for the green brightness at the corner. Slowly, her thoughts loosed their grip and she felt the night. Strange, this clinging dampness for the month of July. A chill crept up her arms and she pulled her coat closer around her. She didn't know where she was going. She just had to go.

The night air was invaded by headlights. Each streak of light swelled and grew as it approached, swallowing up the darkness. Then, with a groan, it was gone, leaving two small red lights sulking behind.

Instinctively, the girl edged away from the street, closer to the grass. With a rush, her thoughts tumbled into their greenness.

"Wish I could crawl up in a tight warm ball, like a cocoon, and emerge a shimmering butterfly, or no, just stay curled up that way, under a leaf, close to the earth, warm and unseen."

Yes, it was quite chilly. She pictured a steaming cup of coffee and herself huddled over the warm vapor-film in a dim back corner. But all the restaurants near here were brightly lit, electric-bulb-bright. Night was warmer than that cold glare.

Store windows she passed seemed sadly empty. Things in them were waiting for morning when the doors opened and the hats marched in and reached for them. Creases shook out of paper bags and money passing into warm hands.

She kept on walking. People passed by her on the street, looking at each other, talking at each other. Sometimes they turned to stare at her, but she scuffled by, head bent.

"They must be wondering where I'm going, in slacks and all, at this hour of the night. I could be going to visit a friend or a maybe a lover ..."

An edginess was prickling in her stomach and squeezing her off the street. It was an emptiness, driven down, that oozed back up into her chest and her throat. A greyness that kept behind her, turning when she turned, following her—or was it inside—a grey mass pushing her. She turned into a back lane.

The bright lights were gone. The lane wound behind the stores and the houses. Trees rose up against the night sky and some hung their branches into the lane, brushing her cheek as she passed. Their leaves quivered and reached out for her. Tenuously, she touched a leaf, feeling its waxy smoothness, and the tree bark, cool and knobbly. Then with a shudder, she was pressed against the bark, arms wrapped tightly around the trunk. Sap seemed to flow into her flesh, melting the emptiness, the yearning. Footsteps scraped behind her but she heard nothing. Body relaxed, eyes closed, she breathed in the deep-lost peacefulness.

When the girl looked up, a face was pressing down at hers and a husky voice whispered: "Hey, baby, looking for some company?"

* * *

The experience of emptiness leads us into a web of darkness woven out of such black thoughts as:

powerlessness, fallibility, error, lack of control, addiction, vulnerability, disease, pain, suffering, death, insensitivity, abuse, injustice, exploitation, greed, envy, deceit, manipulation, distrust, hatred of others, hatred of self.

Trapped in this web, it is easy to fall into deep despair, a despair known in spiritual circles as "the dark night of the soul." We feel cut off from God, from love, and from the light. We are helpless and alone, without comfort, without support, without hope. It is the darkest, blackest place we know. It is the experience of *the Void.*

Moved by this experience of the Void, Sheldon Kopp writes:

Growing up often means facing the anguished isolation of no longer belonging as we wander in exile through a strange world that makes no sense. Each of us must make his or her own way through an indifferent, unfamiliar landscape in which good is not necessarily rewarded, nor evil punished. [85]

Stripped to our basic helplessness, perhaps all we can do is to accept our lot in life. What else is there to do?

> As a grown-up, *ultimately each man is alone.* No man can do for him what he must do for himself.[86]

What we must face, Kopp teaches, is "a life without illusions in a world where there is no appeal." [87]

Even so, we have a choice of whether we do so with an air of weariness or pizzazz. Kopp chooses the latter:

> An unhappy childhood is not a justification for copping out. Life is a mixed bag, at best, for everyone. Each man must face disappointment, frustration, failure, loss and betrayal, illness, aging, and finally his own death. And yet he must face up to Camus' challenge: "*to be a just man in an unjust world.*" You find life arbitrary and yet take things as they are, bring to them what you can, enjoy them as they stand. This is it, often unsatisfying, at times disappointing, always imperfect. But it's the only world we have...[88]

According to this viewpoint, accepting our aloneness, separation, and inevitable death is what it means to grow up and assume a mature approach toward life. The role of the therapist is to point out when we are slipping into childish illusions which serve to shield us from the hard facts of life and then, when we accept these facts, to share with us the common plight of a fellow human being who squarely faces a world without reprieve. As Kopp puts it:

---

85 Kopp, Sheldon, *An End to Innocence: Facing Life Without Illusions*, Bantam Books, New York, 1978, page 4.
86 Kopp, Sheldon B., *Guru: Metaphors From a Psychotherapist*, Science and Behavior Books, Palo Alto, California, 1976, page 203.
87 Kopp, Sheldon: Ibid., page 202.
88 Kopp, Sheldon B., Ibid., page 202.

What I hope to give to my patients - and what I also hope to get from my patients - is the courage and comfort of knowing someone else who faces his life as it is, risks the knowing, feels what I feel, struggles as I struggle, mourns his losses - and survives.[89]

Besides this tough-minded existential stoicism, there is one other possibility - the possibility that we are not as separate and disconnected as we think and that we do not have to manage all by ourselves. Perhaps, instead of being doomed to die alone in a universe that is indifferent to our cries, we are held, supported, and contained in a vast caring field. We get glimpses of this very different possibility from modern physics. As Deepak Chopra points out:

Erwin Schrodinger, who was among the most influential theorists in the early decades of quantum physics, made the conceptual leap that most of us cannot: "Inconceivable as it seems to ordinary reason, you - and all other conscious beings as such - are all in all.".... In other words, you cannot stand anywhere in the universe that is outside yourself. As Schrodinger said, "You are a part of an infinite, eternal being. Thus you can throw yourself flat on the ground, stretched out upon Mother Earth, with the certain conviction that you are one with her and she with you. [90]

Or, again, as Albert Einstein says:

A human being is part of the whole called by us, "universe", a part limited in time and space. He experiences himself, his thoughts and feelings as something separated from the rest, a kind of optical delusion of his consciousness. This delusion is a kind of prison for us, restricting us to our personal desires and to affection for a few persons nearest to us. Our task must be to free ourselves from this prison by widening our circle of compassion to embrace all living creatures and the whole of nature in its beauty.[91]

89 Kopp, Sheldon B., *Guru: Metaphors From a Psychotherapist*, page 204.
90 Chopra, Deepak: *Unconditional Life: Mastering the Forces that Shape Personal Reality*, Bantam Books, New York, 1991, pages 78-79.
91 Einstein, Albert. A personal letter, 1950. (Unconfirmed source)

When we begin to identify with the infinite complexity and harmony of the universe, we no longer feel isolated and alone. We see our place in the vast cosmic scheme and our intimate connection to all that exists. The arms of the universe hold us. We belong; we are at home.

Is this wishful thinking, as Kopp would say, or is Kopp's perspective narrow-minded and myopic, as Einstein would contend? What is truth and what is delusion here? It is a fundamental decision, perhaps *the* most fundamental decision, that each of us will have to make. And it is a decision we have to make for ourselves.

Human beings have pondered and agonized over these questions as far back as our existence goes. What is the meaning of life? Why is there so much pain? Is there a life after death? Is there a purpose to our suffering? Is there an intelligence at work in the universe? Is there a God who cares about us?

Philosophers who put their faith in reason trotted out arguments - "proofs" they were called - to demonstrate the existence of God, while other philosophers debated the validity of these supposed proofs. If such arguments were, indeed, proofs, why the debate? They should have been obvious to anyone. Yet such proofs are convincing to those who already believe in God and consistently fail to move those who do not. Reason, by itself, does not convince.

Mystics, disenchanted with reason, have pointed to their spiritual experience as the only and ultimate "proof" of divine existence. It will, of course, be proof only to those who believe in that experience, while sceptics will continue in their scepticism.

The caterpillar looks up at the butterfly and exclaims: "You'll never get *me* up in one of those things! [92]

If we want to explore for ourselves the spiritual reality

---

92 Ram Dass: "Tuning to the Wisdom Heart: Spiritual Ground for Effective Living", a workshop at Breitenbush Retreat and Conference Centre, Detroit, Oregon, August 1993.

that mystics speak about, there are certain steps that to be followed, certain practices from diverse spiritual traditions that are said to lead the way. These are not offered as "proofs" but as guidelines.

In order to make use of these guidelines, we must be open to the possibility of a spiritual reality and be willing to follow the discipline, often arduous, that is laid out. To the sceptic, this is indulgence in childish illusion, an escape from the hard facts of life. To the devoted, this is a path demanding courage, maturity, and dedication; it is not for the faint of heart.

Who is "right"? Who decides? There is no one "with more seniority" than you yourself.

* * *

I am sitting with black thoughts. Emotional abuse as our daily way of relating; The cycle of abuse passing through generations; Fusion in place of love.

I am thinking about the human condition. The self divided. False self and shadow. Broken trust.

I am sinking into the darkness, the black pit.

Pessimistic conjugation of the verb "to be":

　I am hateful.

　You are hateful.

　The world sucks.

I am contemplating black thoughts. A blue jay flits across my vision and lands on a branch in the back yard. It is a brilliant yellow forsythia in bloom.

* * *

While I have been a therapist for over twenty years, I am not an expert in spirituality. I've read a bit, studied a bit, experienced a bit, and, all in all, I am about Kindergarten level on the path. But I can, at least, point in the direction that a spiritual orientation would take and offer glimpses of what lies in that direction.

When we first encounter the Void, our initial reaction is to contract against it in pain and fear. It feels like a death experience. And yet, if we stay with this experience, "something" survives, some point of consciousness floating, so to speak, in the Void. There is a kind of calmness. The emptiness is soothing. It has a certain spaciousness, even a vibratory quality. It has what feels like *life*.

What is this "something" that senses calmness or who is it that is feeling soothed? It is easier to specify who or what it is *not*. It is not the person we are accustomed to identifying as our self, or our physical being with a certain size and shape. It is not the individual with a particular life history and tendencies to act in a certain way. It is not the person who occupies certain roles in life vis-à-vis other people. It is not a recognizable person at all.

It is apparent, then, that what survives is not the self as we have defined it. The familiar markers are all absent. The ego boundaries have dissolved. There are no object relations. There is no mirroring from other selves. There is no self that is distinct from others. There is no entity which can be identified or defined as separate. There is "nobody" here at all.

Yet there is consciousness, and that consciousness is peaceful. The anguish, the torment is gone. The need for love becomes preposterous. We are in it and we are of it all the time. **Our being *is* love.**

What was our torment becomes a message of compassion. The truth that we discover is:

NOBODY CARES!

This vast nobody, this spaciousness or emptiness or cosmic consciousness, is a loving presence. It is with us all the time. But we in our tight little egos are unaware of it. Thus we think we need what, in reality, we already have. Our neediness is based in the false conviction that we are separate and cut off from love.

The illusion of separateness is the source of our pain. We see ourselves as lonely and isolated egos wandering, as Kopp says, "in exile through a strange world that makes no sense." But what is stark reality for Kopp is an illusion from a spiritual point of view. Indeed, the aim of spiritual training is to free ourselves of precisely the illusion that Kopp regards as truth, the illusion that "ultimately, each man is alone." It is the identification with our solitary ego that causes our feeling of aloneness and our aloneness that causes our pain.

Hugh Prather passes along a story which speaks to this point:

> A man who had finished his life went before God. And God reviewed his life and showed him the many lessons he had learned. When He had finished, God said: "My child, is there anything you wish to ask?" And the man said, "While You were showing me my life, I noticed that when the times were pleasant there were two sets of footprints, and I knew You walked beside me. But when times were difficult there was only one set of footprints. Why, Father, did You desert me during the difficult times?" And God said, "You misinterpret, my son. It is true that when the times were pleasant I walked beside you and pointed out the way. But when the times were difficult, I carried you. [93]

The illusory nature of our separateness is a fundamental spiritual teaching. When we embrace the emptiness, we experience spaciousness. Our neediness dissolves and through the connectedness of all Being, we rediscover love.

On the basis of this spiritual perspective we need to expand our picture. We have moved beyond the confines of our everyday self and beyond our customary modes of maintaining this sense of self. Beyond compliance and defiance, beyond the repressed anger and neediness which compliance and defiance conceal, we encounter the Void.

It is an emptiness that is first experienced with anguish and despair. But if we allow ourselves to stay with this experience,

93 Prather, Hugh: Foreword to Love Is Letting Go of Fear by Gerald G. Jampolsky, Bantam Books Inc., New York, 1970, pages 9-10.

the emptiness becomes peaceful. It is an experience of a spaciousness which dissolves our neediness and fear. We see the illusion of our separateness. We feel one with all that is. With the dissolution of our ego boundaries, we experience ourselves as manifestations of universal love.

The present picture is:

Familiar sense of self

Conscious

False self:

COMPLIANCE   DEFIANCE

----------------------------Unconscious----------------------------

Shadow:

ANGER   NEEDINESS

THE VOID	Scary Emptiness
SPACIOUSNESS	Peaceful Emptiness
CONNECTEDNESS	Recognizing Illusion of Separateness
UNIVERSAL LOVE	

All spiritual approaches carry this same message of universal connectedness and universal love. For instance, *A Course in Miracles* states this principle succinctly:

Teach only love, for that is what you are. [94]

94 Cited in Jampolsky, Gerald G.: *Teach Only Love: The Seven Principles of Attitudinal Healing*, Bantam Books Inc., New York, 1983, page 1.

The same point is expressed at more length by Joan Borysenko:

> You are not alone in your struggles
> nor will you ever be alone.
> From the beginning of time the human heart
> has sought its source in love.
> Guilt is one of many guides back to that source.
>
> We can love and help one another
> only as we have been loved ourselves.
> So the fear, the "sins" of the father
> are visited on the child
> who forgets his birthright of uniqueness and joy
> falling asleep to the love that he is.
>
> The journey of awakening
> is a remembering of Who we really are
> where fear is cured by love
> and the mask we have worn to purchase affection
> melts away in the willingness to rejoice
> in our shadow as well as our light.
>
> Only then can we pick up our power and move on
> to a connectedness with caring, compassion and love
> where we can sing our own songs with joy and thanksgiving
> exulting in our worthiness
> as children of God.[95]

Most of life is dominated by fear and illusion. We are prisoners of our familiar sense of self. We live our lives on the level of ordinary consciousness, skimming along the surface like water beetles, seemingly oblivious to what lies below. We are so busy, so preoccupied, that we forget to look deeper; we do not see beneath the surface of the pond.

---

95 Borysenko, Joan: *Guilt is the Teacher, Love is the Lesson*, Warner Books, Time Warner Company, New York, 1990, page 6.

A poem by E. E. Cummings captures this beetle way of life:

anyone lived in a pretty how town
(with an up so floating many bells down)
spring summer autumn winter
he sang his didn't he danced his did.

Women and men(both little and small)
cared for anyone not at all
they sowed their isn'ts they reaped their same
sun moon stars rain

children guessed(but only a few
and down they forgot as up they grew
autumn winter spring summer)
that noone loved him more by more

when by now and tree by leaf
she laughed his joy she cried his grief
bird by snow and stir by still
anyone's any was all to her

someones married their everyones
laughed their cryings and did their dance
(sleep wake hope and then)they
said their nevers they slept their dream

stars rain sun moon
(and only the snow can begin to explain
how children are apt to forget to remember
with up so floating many bells down)

one day anyone died i guess
(and noone stooped to kiss his face)
busy folk buried them side by side
little by little and was by was

all by all and deep by deep
and more by more they dream their sleep
noone and anyone earth by april
wish by spirit and if by yes.

Women and men(both dong and ding)

summer autumn winter spring
reaped their sowing and went their came
sun moon stars rain [96]

Spirituality is a remembering of that which "children are apt to forget," a going down to recover what we have forgotten as up we grew. How is it that we lose sight of the truth and buy into the illusion? How is it that we forget who we really are?

Ram Dass says that in our ordinary lives, we are all in "somebody training." [97] We are all trying to *be* somebody and *somebody* is who we think we are supposed to be. Our parents think they are somebody, so they teach us to be somebody too. Nobody wants to be "a nobody". Being nobody is like not being seen at all. We want to be seen as "somebody" by other somebodies who will regard us with respect and admiration. To be somebody important or somebody special is our highest aim.

Another poem, one that I memorized with delight many years ago, comes to mind here:

I'm nobody! Who are you?
Are you nobody, too?
Then there's a pair of us - don't tell!
They'd banish us, you know.

How dreary to be somebody!
How public, like a frog
To tell your name the livelong day
To an admiring bog! [98]

By contrast to somebody training, spiritual work is like nobody training. It is a discipline aimed at extricating ourselves from our familiar sense of self, from the illusion of our separateness and of our alienation from love.

How do we learn to be nobody? To dis-identify from the somebody we always thought we were?

96 Cummings, E. E.: *Complete Poems 1913-1962*, Harcourt Brace Jovanovich Inc., New York, 1961, page 515.
97 Ram Dass, "Tuning to the Wisdom Heart". workshop, August 1993.
98 Dickinson, Emily: *Collected Poems*, Courage Books, Running Press, Philadephia, Pennsylvania, 1991, page 97.

Precisely because it is who we *think* we are that gets in our way, one major practice of spiritual work has always been to let go of thinking, to still the chatter of the mind so that we can detach ourselves from thought. This is the practice of *meditation*.

When we are free of thought, we can experience what cannot be thought, pure Being, which is non-conceptual. Pure being is like the sky which is always there, though clouds may block our view. Our thoughts are like clouds, forming and reforming, endlessly. We can choose to focus on the clouds or on the sky. Following this analogy, the words that I am writing right now are like a message spread across a blue sky by a jet stream forming the letters "L-o-o-k -- a-t --t-h-e -- s-k-y." As the letters fade and dissipate, the sky is clear.

As we grow accustomed to meditation, we grow accustomed to stepping back from our reactions and watching them. We become more and more able to look at what is without needing to change it, to feel our pain without running away from it, to observe our reactions without acting them out. We watch with a kind of quiet indifference which we spoke about at the beginning [99] as an open curiosity or unconditional presence. We are neither repelled nor attracted. We simply observe what is.

> Sitting quietly, doing nothing,
> Spring comes, and the grass grows by itself.[100]

Meditation teaches us to dwell in this openness, this spaciousness, so that we can be present without judgment. We can accept without attachment. We can love without need.

We come to realize that who we really are transcends the boundaries of the self as previously conceived. We learn to disidentify from the structures of the personality and to move beyond the limits of the familiar self. We practice detachment.

---

99 c.f. above, Part One, page 15.
100 A Zenrin poem quoted by Alan W. Watts in *The Way of Zen*, Mentor Book published by Pantheon Books Inc., New York , 1957, page 133.

We rest in spaciousness. We simply are.

* * *

When I was at a meditation retreat with Ram Dass, we all went for a walk in the forest. I knew that Ram Dass was walking close behind me. When we set out, I was busily thinking to myself:

"How do you walk in the woods with Ram Dass walking behind you? Do you wiggle? Do you float? Do you pretend that his presence is nothing special? Do you bliss out? How do you walk in the woods knowing that Ram Dass is walking right behind you?"

"You walk the way you would walk in the woods without Ram Dass walking behind you!"

"But if you know he's there behind you, how do you walk as you would walk if you did not know he was there?"

Gradually, I became absorbed in the experience of the forest. I was enraptured by the light. I headed back alone, ahead of the others, drinking in the aliveness, the attunement I felt.

I heard a small rustling noise behind me. As I turned my head, there, just a few inches from my face, I was looking into Ram Dass' eyes. He bent down and kissed me. Then he lightly walked on.

"These lips have been kissed by Ram Dass!" I thought to myself, touching them with reverence. "I'll keep them as a shrine!"

How fickle that, by dinner time, they were eating buttered corn on the cob with great gusto!

* * *

Meditation is a primary method of detaching from our identification with thought. We can also learn to detach by an awareness procedure in which we keep surfacing the identifications we are making and questioning them. We keep asking ourselves "Who am I?" and exploring the answers that emerge.

Almaas explains:

We want to investigate what or who you are taking yourself to be at each moment and question it. Is that really who you are? At each moment there is an identification, there is, in a sense, a feeling of self: "I am watching," or "I am sitting." When you say "I", that "I" is attached to something. Is what you're attaching the "I" to really you?[101]

When we do this exploration, there will be certain kinds of answers that generally come to mind. For example, I may think: I am a middle-aged woman, I am the mother of two boys, I am a therapist, I am five feet four inches tall, I grew up in Forest Hill, I got a Doctorate in Philosophy and taught at the University of Toronto, I became a social worker and a Gestalt therapist, I moved to British Columbia, I fell in love with a psychologist and we bought a house together, I live in that house still, I am sitting at the computer in that house typing these answers right now.

But let us ask with Almaas:

Who is sitting at this moment? Be aware of your experience. See whether you can answer that question. What is it you attach the "I" to? Who am I that is sitting? Most likely you'll see that you attach the "I" to your body. It's the body that is sitting, so when you say "I am sitting", aren't you saying "I am the body"? You're not taking yourself to be a feeling or perception, because feelings don't sit, the mind doesn't walk. The only part that sits, walks, and moves is the body.[102]

What comes to mind first are our identifications with the body: with the shape of the body, the boundaries of the body, the feelings of the body, the memories of the body, the personal history of the body. But let us question further:

When we say "my body," what does the body belong to? Saying "myself" is more accurate, but what exactly does that mean? Who is it who has a body and has a self? Who are you referring to when you say "I have a body"? What is the "I"? It doesn't make sense to say "I have an I" or "self has a self"[103]

---

101 Almaas, A.H., *Diamond Heart Book Three*, page 19.
102 Ibid, page 19.
103 Ibid., page 20.

As we keep questioning, we can step back from each answer we give. As we become aware of the succession of identifications we are making, we can also disengage from them.

> Is it possible to look not only at your body and see your identification with it, but also to look objectively at your personal history without having to identify with it? Is it possible to look at the totality of your personality at once? Most of the time you identify with that totality; you are in the middle of it, as if in a medium like a cloud, and you let the atmosphere of that cloud define you. Is it possible to become aware that you are doing that? Can you look at your experience right now and see how you are identifying with your personal history? [104]

As we disengage, we become aware of the changing nature of our identifications and of a certain arbitrariness about the way we string these identifications together under one label or tag.

> So we see that at different times you take your body to be you, or a feeling to be you, or an essential aspect to be you. Your sense of identity keeps changing its tag. Who you are taking yourself to be shifts all the time. The content is changing but you're always saying "I" as if the "I" were one thing. [105]

When we become aware of the arbitrariness of the labels we use to define ourselves, we can move beyond these labels. When we become aware of the changing process of our identifications, we can detach from and step beyond any identifications we make:

> The moment you become aware of something is the moment of going beyond it. The moment you say, "I am that," you are beyond it. [106]

The implication is that we have moved into an arena beyond

---

104 Ibid., page 23.
105 Ibid., page 25.
106 Ibid., page 28.

definition, beyond conceptualization, beyond words. The very
fact that we formulate an answer means that we transcend that
answer. The act of formulating transcends itself. The awareness
that conceptualizes or defines remains itself forever undefined.

> Maybe you'll just know that you are not defined by anything
> that you usually define yourself with, and that there's no way
> to define yourself. You may only know that you're undefinable,
> and that knowing you are undefinable is freedom. So maybe
> that is the final definition of you. But this is an experience,
> a realization, and not merely a logical conclusion. [107]

The freedom of moving beyond identifications is a freedom
from the past. We no longer need to see ourselves in terms of
what has been true before - old scripts, old patterns, old themes.
We have the ability to detach from our reactivity - that is, from
our attachment to the self we always thought we were. We can
stop seeing ourselves in terms of our history. We can experience
each moment fresh and new without the baggage of the past.

At this point, it becomes clear that spirituality takes a
radical departure from psychotherapy. It is like letting go of all
that we have achieved. The goal of psychotherapy is to learn
to stand behind ourselves - to defend, protect, and advocate
for the self. To be a sympathetic witness to ourselves, we need
to understand the impact of our early history and to recover
the child's perspective on whatever abuse occurred. Through
the process of therapy, we come to identify with that history,
to identify with that child, and to identify with the self in the
totality of its parts. We come to love the self we are identified
with.

Now we discover that the self we have just learned to love
is the self we must let go. From a spiritual perspective, it is our
identification with this self or ego that is the deepest source of
our alienation. It is the self we took such pains to integrate that
is the self we must transcend.

The paradox is that we have to consolidate the self before

---

107 ibid., page 30-31.

we can dismantle it. We have to develop boundaries before we can dissolve them. We have to re-own the past before we can break free of it.

As Almaas says:

> You have to have a self before you can let go of it. When you have a scattered self, it's hard to let go of it. When you have a self that is depressed, scared, or fragmented in some way so that it can't handle reality, you're going to be very busy trying to protect it. You can't possibly allow the openness that would mean a loss of boundaries. [108]

Love is that openness, that loss of boundaries that define the self. From the ego perspective, we are each separate and distinct, like islands that need to be defended and protected. We believe that leaving the island means that we will drown. In this sense, we are all trapped on an island like that child at Camp Kawagama. We are all separate little egos, gazing out at the endless expanse of waves, yearning to go home but afraid that we will drown. Why are we so afraid? From a spiritual perspective, we *are* the ocean; "we are", as Almaas says, "different waves of the same ocean." [109]

How could the ocean drown?

*   *   *

All my life, I have had dreams of packing. Packing boxes, packing suitcases. Whatever I was packing, I could never finish the task. Time and again, I have had the same dreams of packing. To catch a plane, to board a train, to go away somewhere. I never made it. There were always more things to pack. Towering shelves of books or clothes or toys. Things I had forgotten. More boxes or suitcases. I'd turn a corner and there would be more rooms I had not noticed with more things in them. Sometimes a lot, sometimes a little. But always more things to pack.

108 Almaas, A.H.: *Diamond Heart Book Two: The Freedom to Be*, Diamond Books, Almaas Publications, Berkeley, California, 1989, page 147.
109 Ibid., page 147.

My dreams have always ended in the middle of packing. Never finished. Never packed up and ready to go. Always on the verge, almost, but not quite there. Always left with more things to pack.

For years, I have been packing and I never could get packed. What was my problem? What was it that was holding me back? This is the koan my soul has been meditating on.

Where am I leaving?
   Am I trying to leave:
   * camp?
   * my family? (to grow up, face the truth, be autonomous,
     be an adult instead of a child?)
   * my personal history? (the scapegoat role, the victim
     script, the angry abandoned child?)
   * myself ? (my Superego, my perfectionism, my
     self-hate?)
   * life? (suffering, alienation, feeling cut off from love?)
   * the ego? (isolation, aloneness, feeling cut off
     from God?)

Where am I going?
   I am trying to go "home."

What am I packing?
   Too much baggage from the past.

What do I need?
   To let go.

Who am "I" then?
   "I" am a character in a book that is about to end.
   "I" am writing the book.

   "I" am finished.

*   *   *

Postscript

Postscript

This book was finished in 1995. It is now 2009. You may wonder what has changed in the interim. Do I have much the same or a wildly different point of view?

In actuality, I never set out to write a book. I didn't ever think I could. I had some ideas about my work and some stories about my life but I never imagined they would cohere in a whole that would constitute a book like this.

What happened was that I became gripped by a need to write and I just kept on going until the need let go of me. It was like an obsession that took hold of my mind and I had to stay with it. No one was more surprised than I as it grew and grew –from a short presentation to a longer paper to two papers and still there was more, and more, and more.

It had its own energy; its own drive. It consumed every free minute of my time. I would be typing until late at night and scribbling on bits of paper wherever I went during the day. I'd jump up in bed in the middle of the night grasping at a word or a phrase I'd been searching for. I was its captive, its lackey, its slave. I was possessed. Did I write it or did it write me?

Then one night it stopped. You can see exactly how it happened on the last page of Part 7. It just ended abruptly. It was over. I was done.

So it has remained for fourteen years. I have used it in my professional life as material for papers, teaching and therapy but the book sat on the shelf, waiting.

It waited while I moved to a new country. It waited while I raised two sons, both remarkable people with tremendous drive and character of their own. I believe it helped them become who they are because it gave me clarity. We now refer to that clarity in the literature as a "coherent narrative," [110] an understanding that allowed me to parent at my best (which is not to say perfectly).

It waited while I continued to work with hundreds more

---

110 See M. Ainsworth et al., *Patterns of Attachment: A Psychological Study of the Strange Situation*, Erlbaum, Hillsdale, N.J., 1978 and Main, M.: "Attachment Overview with Implications for Clinical Work" in S. Goldberg, R. Muir, and J.Kerr eds. : *Attachment Theory: Social, Developmental and Clinical Perspectives*, Hillsdale, N.,J., Analytic Press, 1995 and their collaboration in the Adult Attachment Interview (1993).

clients who struggled through the journey I had traveled and presented in the book.

While I acquired some high-powered methodology[111] for accessing the unconscious mind and moving people forward in their journeys, the journey is essentially the same. Recent advances in brain imaging and neuropsychology have confirmed the principles in the logic of the therapeutic journey. I believe the theory is essentially sound.

What made me go back to the book then? It was the revolt of my body that prompted me to reopen it after all these years.

I was on a trip with a friend when my body came to a screeching halt. It simply refused to move. All the methods I had developed to deal with the pain of fibromyalgia – the resting, pacing, stretching, self-hypnosis, medications etc. – were of no avail. I came home in a wheel chair.

I was initiated into a new process that both mystified and horrified me. It was as if my body decided it was in its eighties or nineties while my mind was still in its sixties. I was trapped in the body of a very old woman.

Vibrant and active as a person, I struggled to accommodate to a change I could not understand and could not abide. Energy drained out of me. I was forced to spend more and more time horizontal. I cut back my work hours and still came home limp and paralyzed. While I had been used to being busy all morning, afternoon and evening, I shrank to one good period of time each day. There went my evenings out during the week. There went chunks of my social life on weekends. There went long walks on the beach, on the bluffs, in the woods.

I found myself hitting one wall after another. First I had to give up traveling. Then I had to give up gardening. These were the two pillars of my dreamed-of retirement – gone. Nights became an agony and mornings a misery. I had been in pain for seventeen years with fibromyalgia but this took pain to a new level. Instead of whimpering and moaning, my body woke me up screaming. Why was it torturing me?

---

111 I am referring to EMDR which has proven to be the most rapid and effective process-ing method I have experienced or imagined possible.

I went to doctors, chiropractors, acupuncturists, and rheumatologists. No one knew what was going on. And they all said different things: it's muscular/skeletal; it's central nervous system; it's thyroid and adrenals. I followed their advice and got no relief.

I went on a special diet omitting almost every food I liked. I got weaker and lost my appetite but the pain continued, seemingly unimpressed.

I racked my brain for an explanation. I don't know how many hours I spent staring at the ceiling anguishing over my situation. Since I was forced into a more sedentary life style, I tried to think of what on earth I could do to fill all this time I was stuck at home.

That's when I decided to revisit the book. I started editing, keeping faithful to the original text and just making stylistic changes. I was happily editing when my body rebelled again.

First it was frozen shoulders, then it was carpal tunnel, then my hands swelled up so I could not type. We moved the computer, got a new keyboard, tried different positions, used cold compresses, hot baths, and long breaks. My body was unmoved. It did *not* want me to finish this book.

"So what *do* you want?" I asked in desperation. It was 3 a.m. in the calm quiet space that comes after the pain settles down. "I have given up everything I enjoy; everything I value; everything that matters to me in my life. What more do you want of me? There's nothing left to give up."

Aha! I got it. I have been in disengagement training. My body has systematically forced me to give up all my attachments, using pain to pry me loose from everything that bound me to life. When I am ready to move on, this book will remain behind as a kind of legacy of what I have learned and who I have been. I hope it is as helpful to you as it has been to me in making the journey to home.

* * *

Bibliography

Aarons, Rachel B., "The Victim's Journey," *Voices: The Art and Science of Psychotherapy*, Vol. 30, Number 4, Winter 1994.

M. Ainsworth et al., *Patterns of Attachment: A Psychological Study of the Strange Situation*, Erlbaum, Hillsdale, N.J., 1978.

Almaas, A.H.: *Diamond Heart Book One*, Diamond Books, Almaas Publications, Berkeley, 1987.

Almaas, A.H.: *Diamond Heart Book Two: The Freedom to Be*, Diamond Books, Almaas Publications, Berkeley, 1989.

Almaas, A.H., *The Pearl Beyond Price: Integration of Personality into Being: An Object Relations Approach*, Diamond Books, Almaas Publications, first published in 1988, Berkeley

Almaas, A.H.: *Diamond Heart Book Three: Being and the Meaning of Life*, Diamond Books, Almaas Publications, Berkeley, California, 1990.

Bach, George and Wyden, Peter: *The Intimate Enemy*, Avon Books, New York, 1968.

Bach, George and Goldberg, Herbert: *Creative Aggression*, Anchor Doubleday, Garden City, New York, 1983.

Boeckner, Barry: *Angerworks*, Cambridge Interfaith Family Counselling Centre, Cambridge, Ontario, 1993.

Birnbaum, Jack: *Cry Anger: A Cure for Depression*, General Publishing, Don Mills, Ontario, 1973.

Blake, William: "Songs of Innocence" and "Songs of Experience in *William Blake*, Introduced and Edited by J. Bronowski, Penguin Books, Harmondsworth, Middlesex, England, 1958.

Borysenko, Joan: *Guilt is the Teacher, Love is the Lesson*, Warner Books, New York, 1990.

Bradshaw, John: *Healing the Shame That Binds You*, Health Communications, Deerfield Beach, Florida, 1988.

Bradshaw, John: *Homecoming: Reclaiming and Championing Your Inner Child*, Bantam Books, New York, 1992.

Buber, Martin: *I & Thou*, Charles Scribner's Sons, New York, 1958.

Cary, Joyce: *The Horse's Mouth*, M. Joseph, London, 1944.

Cashdan, Sheldon: *Object Relations Therapy*, W. W. Norton, New York, 1988.

Cheek, David and LeCron Leslie: *Clinical Hypnotherapy*, Grune & Stratton, A Subsidiary of Harcourt Brace Jovanovich Publishers, New York, 1968.

Chopra, Deepak: *Unconditional Life: Mastering the Forces that Shape Personal Reality*, Bantam Books, New York, 1991.

Cummings, E.E.: *Complete Poems 1913-1962*, Harcourt Brace Jovanovich Inc., New York, 1961.

Dickinson, Emily: *Collected Poems*, Courage Books, Running Press, Philadelphia, Pennsylvania, 1991.

Feldmar, Andrew: "Children and Morality", a lecture presented in Vancouver, British Columbia, March 1993.

Firestone, Robert: *The Fantasy Bond*, Human Sciences Press, New York, 1987.

Forward, Susan, *Obsessive Love*, Bantam Books, Toronto, June 1992

Freud, Sigmund: Civilization and Its Discontents, (translated by James Strachey), W.W. Norton & Co. Inc., New York, 1961

Gawain, Shakti: *Reflections in the Light: Daily Thoughts and Affirmations*, New World Library, San Rafael, California, 1988.

Gendlin, Eugene T.: *Focusing*, 2nd edition, Bantam Books, New York, 1981.

Goldberg, Jane: *The Dark Side of Love*, G. P. Putman's Sons, New York, 1993.

Gordon, Lori H.: *Passage to Intimacy*, Simon & Schuster Inc., New York, 1993.

Jampolsky, Gerald G.: *Teach Only Love: The Seven Principles of Attitudinal Healing*, Bantam Books Inc., New York, 1983.

Jung, Carl: *Modern Man in Search of a Soul*, Harcourt, Brace & World, New York, first published in 1933.

Collected Works of C.G. Jung, Pantheon Books, New York, 1954.

Kant, Immanuel: *Foundations of the Metaphysics of Morals*, (translated by L.W. Beck), Indiapolis, 1970.

Karpman, Stephen B: "Fairy Tales and Script Drama Analysis", Transactional Analysis Bulletin, VII, No. 26 (April 1968).

Katharine, Anne: *Boundaries: Where You End and I Begin*,

Parkside Publishing Company, Park Ridge, Illinois, 1991.

Kopp, Sheldon B.: *Guru: Metaphors From a Psychotherapist*, Science and Behavior Books, Palo Alto, California, 1976.

Kopp, Sheldon: *An End to Innocence: Facing Life Without Illusions*, Bantam Books, New York, 1978.

Laing: R.D.: *Knots*, Penguin Books, Middlesex, England, 1970.

Levine, Stephen: *Who Dies?*, Anchor Doubleday, New York, 1982.

Lowen, Alexander: *Love and Orgasm*, Macmillan, New York, 1965, *The Betrayal of the Body*, Macmillan, New York, 1967, *The Language of the Body*, Macmillan, New York, 1971, *Bioenergetics*, Penguin Books, New York, 1975.

Main, M.: "Attachment Overview with Implications for Clinical Work" in S. Goldberg, R. Muir, and J.Kerr,eds. : Attachment Theory: Social, Developmental and Clinical Perspectives, Hillsdale, N.J., Analytic Press, 1995.

Mayer, Mercer: *There's A Nightmare in My Closet*, Dial Books for Young Readers, E.P. Dutton, New York 1968.

Miller, Alice: *The Drama of the Gifted Child*, Basic Books, New York, 1982; *For Your Own Good: Hidden Cruelty in Childrearing and the Roots of Violence*, The Noonday Press, New York. 1990; *The Untouched Key: Tracing Childhood Trauma in Creativity and Destructiveness*, Doubleday, New York, 1990; *Banished Knowledge: Facing Childhood Injuries*, Doubleday, New York, 1990; *Breaking Down the Wall of Silence: The Liberating Experience of Facing Painful Truth*, A Dutton Book, The Penguin Group, New York, 1991.

Mindell, Arnold: *Working With the Dreaming Body*, Arkana published by the Penguin Group, London, 1989.

Mindell, Arnold and Amy: *Riding the Horse Backwards: Process Work in Theory and Practice*, Arkana published by the Penguin Group, London, 1992.

Moseley, Doug and Naomi: *Dancing in the Dark: The Shadow Side of Intimate Relationships*, North Star Publications, Georgetown, Massachusetts, 1994.

Orwell, George: *Nineteen Eighty-Four*, first published by Martin

Secker & Warburg, 1949, published in Penguin Books, London, 1954.

Paul, Jordan and Margaret: *Do I Have to Give Up Me to Be Loved By You?* CompCare Publishers, Minneapolis, Minnesota, 1983.

Peck, M. Scott: *People of the Lie*, Simon & Schuster Inc., New York, 1983.

Perls, Frederick: *Gestalt Therapy Verbatim*, Bantam Books, New York, 1969.

The Essential Piaget, (ed. Howard Gruber and J. Jacques Voneche,) Basic Books, New York, 1977.

Prather, Hugh: Foreword to *Love Is Letting Go of Fear* by Gerald G. Jampolsky, Bantam Books Inc., New York, 1970.

Ram Dass: *On Relationships*, (audiotape) Windstar Series, The Soundworks, Arlington, Virginia, 1984.

Ram Dass: *Tuning to the Wisdom Heart: Spiritual Ground for Effective Living*, a workshop at Breitenbush Retreat and Conference Centre, Detroit, Oregon, August 1993.

Ray, Sondra: *I Deserve Love: How Affirmations Can Guide You to Personal Fulfillment*, Celestial Arts, Berkeley, California, 1976.

Reich, William: *The Function of the Orgasm*, Orgone Institute Press, New York, 1942.

Rilke, Rainer Maria: *Duino Elegies*, (translated by David Young,) W.W. Norton & Company, New York, 1978

Rogers, Carl: *On Becoming a Person*, Houghton Mifflin, Boston, 1961; *Freedom to Learn*, Charles E. Merrill, Columbus, Ohio, 1969, "Client-Centered Psychotherapy" in *Comprehensive Textbook of Psychiatry*, Vol. 11, Willams & Wilkins, Baltimore, 1975.

Rubin, Theodore Isaac: *Compassion and Self-Hate: An Alternative to Despair*, Collier Books, New York, 1975 and *The Angry Book*, Collier Books, New York, 1970.

Sams, Jamie & Carson, David: *Medicine Cards: The Discovery of Power Through the Ways of Animals*, Bear & Company, Sante Fe, New Mexico, 1988.

Sartre, Jean Paul: *Being and Nothingness, A Phenomenological Essay on Ontology,* (translated by Hazel E. Barnes,) Citadel Press, New York, 1956.

Satir, Virginia: *Conjoint Family Therapy,* Science & Behavior Books, Palo Alto, 1967 *and Peoplemaking,* Science and Behavior Books, Palo Alto, 1972.

Sellnor, Judith A and James G., *Loving for Life: Your self-help guide to a successful, intimate relationship,* Self- Counsel Press, Psychology Series, 2nd edition, May 1991

Shengold, Leonard: *Soul Murder: The Effects of Childhood Abuse and Deprivation,* Fawcett Columbine, New York, 1989.

Spitz, Rene: *The First Year of Life,* International Universities Press, New York 1965.

Stephens, Wallace: *Collected Poems,* Alfred Knopf, New York, 1954.

Tolkien, J.R.R.: *Lord of the Rings,* Part Two: The Two Towers, Ballantine Books, New York, 1965.

Truax, C.B., "A Scale for the Rating of Accurate Empathy" in C.R. Rogers, E.T. Gendlin, D.J. Kiesler & C.B. Truax (Eds.), *The Therapeutic Relationship and its Impact: A Study of Psychotherapy with Schizophrenics,* University of Wisconsin Press, Madison, Wisconsin, 1967.

Watkins, Helen H.: "The Silent Abreaction", *The International Journal of Clinical and Experimental Hypnosis,* 1980, Vol. XXVlll, No. 2.

Watkins, John G., "The Affect Bridge: A Hypnoanalytic Technique," *The International Journal of Clinical and Experimental Hypnosis,* 1971 Vol. XlX No. 1.

Watts, Alan W.: *The Way of Zen,* Mentor Book published by Pantheon Books Inc., New York, 1957.

Welwood, John: "Psychotherapy and the Power of Truth", *Yoga Journal,* May/June 1992.

Woolf, Virginia: *A Room of One's Own,* Flamingo, An Imprint of Harper Collins Publishers, Hammersmith, London, 1984.

About The Author

Rachel B. Aarons, MSW, PhD, began her professional career as a philosopher. She was awarded numerous scholarships and fellowships including the prestigious Woodrow Wilson National Fellowship, the Horace B. Rackham Graduate Prize Fellowship, and the Canada Council Dissertation Fellowship. She completed her Doctorate in Philosophy at the University of Michigan in 1971 and then taught at the University of Toronto as a Lecturer and Assistant Professor of Philosophy from 1968 to 1973.

At this point, her career took a new direction. She received a Master's degree in clinical social work from the University of Toronto and also completed a 3 year training program as a Gestalt therapist at the Gestalt Therapy Institute of Toronto. She opened her private practice in Toronto, which she maintained until moving to Vancouver, BC, in 1978. She was also trained by Virginia Satir as a conjoint family therapist and later became a Faculty member of the Northwest Satir Institute.

In Vancouver, Dr. Aarons founded and coordinated a women's resource center and also served as a career counselor for Capilano University before she returned to private practice in Counseling and Hypnotherapy in 1984.

Dr. Aarons moved to Santa Barbara, California, in 1996 and was licensed as a Clinical Social Worker for the State of California (LCS 18298) in 1997. She was first trained in EMDR in 1998 and became certified as an EMDR therapist in 2004. She continued her practice as a therapist first under the auspice of the Family Therapy Institute of Santa Barbara and then in her own private practice. For over thirty years, Dr. Rachel Aarons has been a companion and guide to individuals and couples on their journeys to growth and healing.

Contact Information:

Dr. Rachel B. Aarons, LCSW
1018 Garden Street, Suite 106, Santa Barbara, CA 93101
Tel. (805) 450-6365 Fax: (805) 617-1700
Email: rbaarons@yahoo.com, - Website: www.RachelAarons.com

Breinigsville, PA USA
29 October 2009
226683BV00002B/2/P